Abraham Lincoln: A Living Legacy

A Guide to Three Abraham Lincoln National Park Sites:

- Abraham Lincoln Birthplace National Historic Site
- Lincoln Boyhood National Memorial
- Lincoln Home National Historic Site

D0011482

Using This Handbook
The three historic sites preserved and maintained by the National Park Service provide insight into the birth, boyhood and remarkable life of Abraham Lincoln. Part 1 of this handbook tells the story of his birth in a log cabin in Kentucky and how the site became Abraham Lincoln Birthplace National Historic Site. Part 2 describes the journey from Kentucky to Indiana, where his father, Thomas, brought young Abraham and the other members of this pioneer family in search of a more secure life, and the ultimate preservation of Lincoln Boyhood National Memorial. Part 3 explores Lincoln's life in Illinois as husband, father, friend, lawyer, state leader and finally president, where, at Lincoln Home National Historic Site, both the Lincoln home and neighborhood are preserved much as they appeared in Lincoln's time. Finally, an appendix provides readers with a list of other sites that provide additional historical perspective on the life of Abraham Lincoln.

On the cover: Reproduction of painting by J. L. G. Ferris, Library of Congress image

Abraham Lincoln Birthplace National Historic Site, Lincoln Boyhood National Memorial, and Lincoln Home National Historic Site are among over 390 parks in the National Park System. The National Park Service cares for these special places saved by the American people so that all may experience our heritage. To learn more about national parks and National Park Service programs in America's communities, visit www.nps.gov. Or visitors can find out more about the three sites featured here by contacting them directly, as indicated below:

Abraham Lincoln Birthplace National Historic Site
2995 Lincoln Farm Road
Hodgenville, KY 42748 - 9707
270-358-3137
www.nps.gov/abli

Lincoln Boyhood National Memorial
2916 E. South Street
Lincoln City, IN 47552
812-937-4541
www.nps.gov/libo

Lincoln Home National Historic Site
413 S. Eighth Street
Springfield, IL 62701-1905
217-391-3221
www.nps.gov/liho

HON. ABRAHAM LINCOLN,

"OUR NEXT PRESIDENT".

Published by Currier & Ives, 152 Nassau St. N.Y.

Introduction

By Frank J. Williams

Abraham Lincoln was born February 12, 1809, in a one-room log cabin on the Sinking Spring farm near Hodgenville, Kentucky. In 1816, the Lincoln family moved to Indiana, where Abraham remained until 1830. Illinois then became his home. The environment in which he lived in Kentucky, Indiana and Illinois, as this guidebook amply demonstrates, nurtured a life that was to have a profound and lasting influence on American civilization.

Knowing little about his family history, Lincoln displayed little interest in it. Instead he became a self-made man in the truest sense of the term; his own life could speak for itself without reference to his ancestors. That was part of the American dream. In 1860 when he was receiving serious consideration as the Republican presidential candidate, the public knew very little about him. The editor of the *Chicago Press and Tribune* sent John Locke Scripps to Springfield to gather information for a short campaign biography. Scripps encountered difficulty when he informed Lincoln of his mission. "Why, Scripps, it is a great piece of folly to attempt to make anything out of my early life. It can all be condensed into a simple sentence, and that sentence you will find in "Gray's Elegy," 'The short and simple annals of the poor.' That's my life, and that's all you or any one else can make of it."

As a result, many members of the new Republican Party felt another Republican should be elected president rather than Lincoln. Few people—including many neighbors of Lincoln's youth in Kentucky, Indiana and Illinois—believed that the uneducated and inexperienced Lincoln was capable of providing the necessary leadership as chief magistrate. But, in his biography of Lincoln, the poet Carl Sandburg sums up those years of the boy Lincoln's pioneer existence as "part of something bigger." This guidebook explores the spirit of those foundational years for America's sixteenth president.

Currier & Ives published this engraving, entitled "Hon. Abraham Lincoln: 'Our Next President'" in 1860, the year he was elected.

Frank J. Williams is Chief Justice of the Rhode Island Supreme Court. He is founding-Chair of The Lincoln Forum and a member of the U.S. Abraham Lincoln Bicentennial Commission.

Part 1

Wall
1931

Lincoln in Kentucky

Through the Cumberland Gap

By Sandra Brue, Chief of Interpretation,
Abraham Lincoln Birthplace National Historic Site

"It was no accident that planted Lincoln on a Kentucky farm. If the Union was to be saved it had to be a man of such an origin that should save it."

— Mark Twain

Preceding pages: *No photo or other image exists from Lincoln's childhood. This illustration by Bernard Wall depicts the frontier time period.*

Architect John Russell Pope designed a dramatic approach to the Memorial Building at the Abraham Lincoln Birthplace National Historic Site. Fifty-six steps, one for each year of Lincoln's life, lead visitors up to the six-column Doric portico.

Abraham Lincoln, our country's sixteenth president, was born in Hardin County (now LaRue County), Kentucky, but his story begins in Virginia with the early wilderness explorers—Dr. Thomas Walker and Daniel Boone. President Lincoln was named for his paternal grandfather, a true pioneer and good friend of Boone. The senior Abraham Lincoln, who could trace his ancestry to English immigrants, had Quaker roots. As Quakers, the Lincolns may have experienced some religious persecution in Massachusetts. A desire for religious freedom may have driven them westward where there was also abundant opportunity for land in Virginia.

Ida Tarbell, a renowned biographer and journalist, began a lifelong search for the Lincoln family's heritage in 1895, as she "ran down the records that had been left behind." Tarbell followed the Lincolns from their roots in Massachusetts to Virginia. In 1770, six years before the Declaration of Independence, Abraham senior was living in the Shenandoah Valley, where he married Bersheba Herring, a member of one of the first families of Rockingham County, Virginia. Abraham, whom Bersheba married against her family's wishes, was described as "a poor and rather plain man." But Tarbell found that Abraham and Bersheba had become extensive property owners in Virginia and accumulated a record for local service. Abraham served as captain in the militia and as judge advocate of the court. The couple had five children: three sturdy boys and two girls. There were many opportunities here, and Jacob, Abraham's brother, remained in Virginia and prospered. However, like their friend Daniel Boone, Abraham and Bersheba were filled with the migratory spirit of those moving west. The family joined the thousands of others who surged through the Cumberland Gap, the break in the formidable Appalachian mountain chain discovered by Dr. Thomas Walker in 1750.

Despite great risks—Daniel Boone had already lost his son during an earlier adventure—in 1782, the senior Abraham Lincoln sold his extensive Virginia farm. He and his wife Bersheba, their sons Mordecai,

11

Visitors to the Abraham Lincoln Birthplace National Historic Site can walk in the footsteps of Lincoln as a very young child. The figures shown here and on exhibit at the birthplace site portray Thomas, Nancy, two-year-old Sarah, and baby Abraham about the time of his first birthday. The park has two locations: the birthplace where the Lincoln family lived from 1808 to 1811; and his boyhood home at Knob Creek, where they lived from 1811 to 1816. At the historic site, visitors can learn about the symbolic cabin at the Memorial Building, visit the Knob Creek site, take advantage of park facilities, enjoy the trails, and view the historic Sinking Spring.

In 1782 Abraham Lincoln (grandfather of President Lincoln) brought his family through the Cumberland Gap into Kentucky, which was still part of Virginia at the time. The official peace treaty ending the Revolutionary War with England was not signed until 1783. Kentucky entered the Union as the fifteenth state in 1792.

"Where many were, but few remain Of old familiar things . . . ."

—A. Lincoln, from "My Childhood Home"

Josiah, and Thomas, and daughters Nancy and Mary, followed Lincoln's great friend Daniel Boone down the Wilderness Road through the Cumberland Gap into "Kentuckee."

Within a few years, the Lincoln family owned more than five thousand acres near Long Run in what is now Jefferson County, some of the richest soil in Kentucky. But the senior Abraham would meet the same fate as other doomed settlers. In 1786, just four years after settling in this new land, Abraham Lincoln was working the fields with his three sons one day when, as the boys watched in horror, an American Indian shot and mortally wounded him. Thomas was ten years old and Mordecai was about fifteen. While young Thomas Lincoln, future father of the president, stooped over his father's body, his brother Mordecai shot the Indian. Today, in the community of Eastwood, along U.S. 60 in Jefferson County, a gravestone-sized marker identifies the general location where the grandfather of the future president fell.

The shot that killed his father was a turning point in young Thomas Lincoln's life, defining it as one of struggle for everything he ever owned. Mordecai Lincoln, the oldest son, inherited their father's entire estate. Sometime later, Bersheba moved her children to Washington County, Kentucky, where young Thomas grew up in the shadow of his oldest brother. Thomas lived with his mother Bersheba until her death in 1793. Afterward, he probably lived near or with his brother Mordecai in Washington County, where his brother Josiah also owned an adjoining farm.

There is no indication that Thomas Lincoln ever resented his brothers' good fortune or spent much time brooding over his fate. Lacking any property, Thomas turned to carpentry, apprenticed himself as a carpenter in Elizabethtown, and soon excelled in cabinetmaking. He did so well that in 1803 he purchased a 238-acre farm on Mill Creek, twelve miles north of his Elizabethtown shop on the tributary of Salt River. However, he apparently never lived on the property or farmed the fields, for it seems he spent most of his time in carpentry work.

Settling near his brothers provided at least one happy ending for young Thomas. The Lincoln brothers' farms bordered on that of Richard and Rachel Berry, who shared their home with their niece, Nancy Hanks. A native Virginian like Thomas, Nancy was born in 1784, the daughter of Lucy Shipley and James Hanks. When Nancy's father died, her mother moved with other family members to Kentucky. Lucy Shipley Hanks later married Henry Sparrow. For reasons unknown, Nancy went to live in Washington County

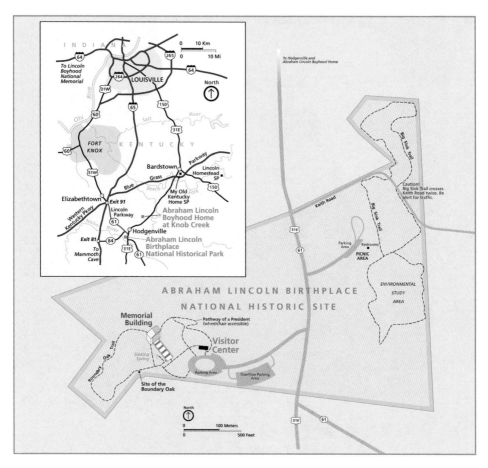

with her mother's sister, Rachel Shipley Berry, and her husband, Richard Berry. On June 12, 1806, Nancy Hanks wed Thomas Lincoln in Springfield, Kentucky, part of Washington County where they had both grown up. Reverend Jesse Head performed the marriage ceremony, a simple but pleasant affair, with a dinner, and friends and neighbors from far and wide.

After their wedding, Nancy and Thomas set up housekeeping in Elizabethtown near his carpenter shop and in the vicinity of Mill Creek farm. In February 1807, a daughter, Sarah, was born. In December 1808, he and Nancy purchased another property, the 300-acre Sinking Spring farm, from Isaac Bush for $200 cash. The farm, located about fourteen miles from Elizabethtown near Hodgen's Mill, was named for the spring flowing year-round with fresh water so vital for livestock, farming and, most importantly, the family's needs for drinking, cooking and bathing.

With Sarah nearly two years old, and with Nancy expecting their second child, the growing Lincoln family settled into their cozy cabin, nestled somewhere

The Abraham Lincoln Birthplace National Historic Site consists of two units: the Birthplace unit, three miles south of Hodgenville on U.S. 31E; and the Boyhood Home unit, also on U.S. 31E, ten miles northeast of the Birthplace site.

15

The Lincolns typified families who settled on the Kentucky frontier in the early 1800s. While there are no photos of Lincoln as a boy, Carl Howell, the owner of the nearby Nancy Lincoln Inn, commissioned artist Lloyd Ostendorf to create this scene of the Lincoln family, including two-year-old Abraham holding his father's hand. Thomas and Nancy's marriage certificate *(far left)*—found after Lincoln's death—lays to rest the long-debated question of whether Lincoln was born in Kentucky as well as his legitimacy. The certificate, signed by Reverend Jesse Head in Washington County, Kentucky, reads in part: "I have Solemnized the rites of Matrimony between Thomas Lincoln and Nancy Hanks: June 12th 1806 AD...." Exhibits at the historic site help visitors imagine life centered around the hearth of the one-room cabin.

Westward Progress
of the Lincoln Family

The story of the Lincoln family migration actually begins in Massachusetts, where Abraham Lincoln senior, Abraham's grandfather, had Quaker roots. A desire for religious freedom and the abundance of land may have driven them westward.

> "The hard condition of his early life…only gave greater life, vigor, and buoyancy to the heroic spirit of Abraham Lincoln."
>
> —Frederick Douglass

in the vicinity of a knoll by the Sinking Spring near Hodgen's Mill for which Hodgenville would eventually be named. Their neighbors were the Brownfields, the Creals, the Enlows, and another of Nancy's aunts and uncles, Thomas and Betsy Sparrow. Living with the Sparrows was Nancy's cousin, Dennis Hanks. Neither were they isolated from family and friends, unlike other pioneer families, with Elizabethtown just fourteen miles north.

Although their new home was tiny (likely no more than 16-by-18 feet), items they brought from Elizabethtown made the new home comfortable. Thomas' skills as a carpenter provided furniture for the family and for sale to other settlers, while Nancy's abilities as a spinner and weaver provided clothing for her husband and young children. They also still owned the Mill Creek farm, and Thomas' business would have called him to the Hardin County seat of government from time to time, where he purchased store-bought items they could not produce for themselves. Like other settlers, Thomas planted corn, beans, squash, and pumpkins and whatever else was needed to sustain his family. He likely also had a few head of livestock. Although the work was demanding, the first two years were good.

Their future was bright when a son, Abraham, named for his grandfather, was born February 12, 1809. Dennis Hanks, Lincoln's older cousin, recalled the morning of Lincoln's birth. He remembered Thomas coming to the cabin of Nancy's aunt and uncle to announce, "Nancy has a boy." Hanks ran for the nearby cabin and found Nancy lying on a pole bed with baby Abraham cuddled near her. To keep

In December 1808, Thomas and Nancy Lincoln settled on Sinking Spring farm near Hodgen's Mill. Abraham was born there two months later. Thomas likely chose to purchase the farm in part because of this dependable water source where young Lincoln probably took his first drink. Travelers such as those shown above around 1910 *(inset photo)* often stopped at the spring to drink the cool, clear water. Modern travelers still pause at the spring preserved at the Lincoln Birthplace site.

In 1894, businessman Alfred Dennett purchased the Sinking Spring farm where Lincoln was born and attempted to bring people to the remote location with plans for a hotel and park. But his efforts failed, so in 1897 he dismantled the cabin pictured here, originally thought to be Lincoln's birthplace. He took it on tour with another cabin described as the birthplace of Jefferson Davis. The logs were displayed during the 1901 Pan-American Exposition in Buffalo, New York. After the exhibit, the logs were put into storage in College Point, Long Island. Dennett went bankrupt and Richard Lloyd Jones, an editor for *Collier's Weekly* as well as a member of and agent for the Lincoln Farm Association, purchased 110 acres of the Sinking Spring farm in 1906 at a public auction for $3,600. The Lincoln Farm Association was established in 1906 to honor and perpetuate Lincoln's memory.

Shortly after the association purchased the farm, they launched a search for the "original birthplace cabin." A report in *Collier's Weekly* dated February 10, 1906, stated that the cabin was being "held for ransom" by Dennett. In truth, the disassembled cabin had been stored at College Point, Long Island, after Dennett became incapacitated. The association purchased the logs for $1,000 and brought them back to Kentucky for storage until the centennial celebration. In the inset photo at center, workers load logs from the cabin onto a horse-drawn wagon at College Point, N.Y., on February 21, 1906, in preparation for shipment to Hodgenville, Kentucky, for reassembly at Lincoln's birthplace.

Despite the association's diligent investigations at the time of their purchase and subsequent assurances that the logs were original, questions swirled regarding their authenticity. It was not until scholar Roy Hays published an article titled, "Is the Lincoln Birthplace Cabin Authentic?" in the *Abraham Lincoln Quarterly* in 1949 that scholarly research began. But it would take another fifty-five years and emerging technology to finally put the question to rest.

In 2004, scientists, or dendrochronologists, who specialize in tree-ring dating determined through core samples that the logs dated only to the 1840s—too new to be the original cabin. Nonetheless for more than a century, the old cabin played a significant role in perpetuating the image of Lincoln's dramatic rise from humble beginnings to the White House. Today, in light of this role and the respectful manner with which the Lincoln Farm Association treated it, the same cabin now stands on the rise above the spring on the spot where Lincoln was born. Sheltered by and in sharp contrast to the elegant Memorial Building, it endures as a symbol of the birthplace and life of this modest man who rose to lead and reunite the nation.

Today young guests at the visitor center of the Abraham Lincoln Birthplace National Historic Site can recreate typical pioneer buildings using Lincoln Logs™. First manufactured in 1916 just a few years after the centennial of Lincoln's birth and named for the beloved sixteenth president, the perpetually popular Lincoln Logs™ originally came with instructions on how to build Lincoln's log cabin.

Early surveyors frequently used less than perfect techniques, poor math skills, and impermanent trees, rocks, and creeks as survey markers, and sent their surveys to the land office in Richmond, Virginia, the state capitol, prior to Kentucky statehood in 1792. Poor penmanship, overlapping surveys, and lost shipments of the bundled survey batches further complicated ownership. Sinking Spring farm bears witness to these uncertain survey methods. An 1837 survey identified the farm's boundary as "at a large white oak thirteen poles above the Sinking Spring or Rock Spring." It was even a principal identifying feature in the deed of conveyance of Abraham Lincoln Birthplace National Historic Site to the United States in 1916. Today a stump marks the site of the Boundary Oak, described as a "large white oak" highlighted in the 1807 Sinking Spring farm survey pictured here. This living link to Abraham Lincoln stood less than 150 yards from the cabin where he was born, and was thought to be twenty-five to thirty years old at the time of Lincoln's birth. It is pictured here as it appeared in 1938. Time, weather, insects, and disease took their toll on this tree that was 6 feet in diameter and 90 feet high with a crown spread of 115 feet when it was taken down in 1986.

them warm that cold February morning, Thomas had thrown a bear skin over the pair before leaving the house. Unfortunately a protracted land dispute would soon cost them their idyllic life on the farm at Sinking Spring.

In 1786, Richard Mather, a land speculator from New York, had purchased a large tract of land that included the Sinking Spring farm. He sold the 300-acre Sinking Spring portion to David Vance in 1805, with an agreement that Mather would hold a lien on the land until the entire sum was paid in full. That same year, Vance signed the bond over to Isaac Bush, who then signed it over to Thomas Lincoln. The debt still unpaid, Mather brought suit against Vance, Bush, and the Lincolns on September 1, 1813. On September 12, 1816, after a lengthy court battle, the Hardin Circuit Court found in favor of Mather, and the land was auctioned. While it was a terrible loss, Thomas had foreseen the possible outcome and had moved his family to Knob Creek two years before the escalating land dispute went to court.

The Lincoln family Bible, printed in 1799, was perhaps the first book that Abraham Lincoln saw. It is part of the collection at Abraham Lincoln Birthplace National Historic Site.

Knob Creek farm: Lincoln's boyhood home

Historians question why the Lincoln family did not move back to Elizabethtown, where they owned the Mill Creek farm, instead of leasing land in the Knob Creek Valley, at the foot of Muldraugh's Hill, around 1811. It is possible the title for the Elizabethtown property was also in question, a common dilemma in Kentucky due to the uncertain survey methods of the time. The first indication that the Lincolns had moved to Knob Creek was notice of a stray horse found near the Knob Creek farm published May 11, 1811, by Thomas Lincoln. The Lincolns had leased thirty acres of bottomland from George Lindsey adjoining that of George Redmon, one of the largest landowners in the area. The soil was rich, but there were fewer acres to farm than at Sinking Spring because of the steep limestone cliffs and deep woods that lined the valley.

"My earliest recollection, … is of the Knob Creek place," Lincoln wrote in a June 4, 1860, letter to Samuel Haycraft, the circuit clerk in Elizabethtown, Kentucky. During a conversation in the White House, President Lincoln once remarked that, "I remember the old home very well. Our farm was composed of three fields, which lay in a valley surrounded by high hills and deep gorges. Sometimes when there came a big rain in the hills the water would come down the gorges and spread over the farm. The last thing I

"[The Bible] is 'the best gift God has given to man.'"

— A. Lincoln

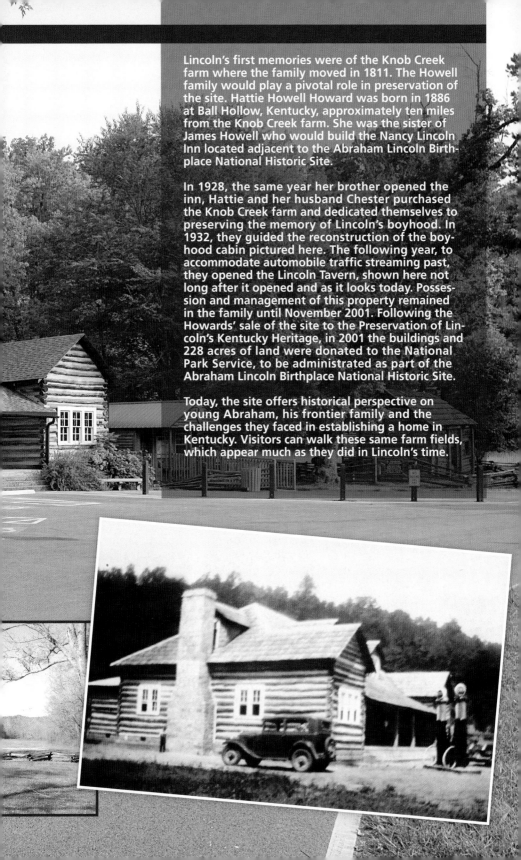

Lincoln's first memories were of the Knob Creek farm where the family moved in 1811. The Howell family would play a pivotal role in preservation of the site. Hattie Howell Howard was born in 1886 at Ball Hollow, Kentucky, approximately ten miles from the Knob Creek farm. She was the sister of James Howell who would build the Nancy Lincoln Inn located adjacent to the Abraham Lincoln Birthplace National Historic Site.

In 1928, the same year her brother opened the inn, Hattie and her husband Chester purchased the Knob Creek farm and dedicated themselves to preserving the memory of Lincoln's boyhood. In 1932, they guided the reconstruction of the boyhood cabin pictured here. The following year, to accommodate automobile traffic streaming past, they opened the Lincoln Tavern, shown here not long after it opened and as it looks today. Possession and management of this property remained in the family until November 2001. Following the Howards' sale of the site to the Preservation of Lincoln's Kentucky Heritage, in 2001 the buildings and 228 acres of land were donated to the National Park Service, to be administrated as part of the Abraham Lincoln Birthplace National Historic Site.

Today, the site offers historical perspective on young Abraham, his frontier family and the challenges they faced in establishing a home in Kentucky. Visitors can walk these same farm fields, which appear much as they did in Lincoln's time.

The distinguished Americans listed on this plaque located on the rear of the Memorial Building formed the Lincoln Farm Association to preserve the farm where Lincoln was born and to build a memorial to his legacy.

remember doing there was one Saturday afternoon; the other boys planted the corn in what we called the 'big field'—it contained seven acres—and I dropped the pumpkin seed." He recalled that a heavy rain came that next week and washed out all the seeds, which had to be replanted.

Except for the few remarks such as these that Lincoln made about his early life, little is known of the family who lived at the foot of Muldraugh's Hill from 1811 until they departed for Indiana in 1816. When asked for a biographic sketch to assist with his 1860 campaign, the humble Lincoln was brief: "There is not much of it, for the reason, I suppose, that there is not much of me."

As it was most likely with their first cabin, their new home offered a single room with one door, a window, and sleeping loft. It sat near a major road that would become U.S. 31E. In 1811 this road that brought the world to their front door was called the Bardstown and Green River Turnpike. Along this road, young Sarah and Abraham likely watched peddlers calling out on foot or from their ramshackle wagons rattling with wares, goods carried to market, soldiers coming home from the War of 1812, and slaves going about their master's business. While living at Knob Creek, the children attended the "ABC" school, taught by Zachariah Riney and later Caleb Hazel, one of the few structured periods of Abraham's education. He later stated that his formal education totaled only one year. Yet surely these experiences and the instruction he received during this time would become a significant part of the later policies and politics of the future president.

Thomas frequently traveled from Knob Creek to Elizabethtown to serve on juries, appraise his neighbors' estates, attend estate sales, and, most importantly, defend himself in Richard Mather's lawsuit. The lawsuit was not their only heartache. During their time at Knob Creek, a third child—a son named for his father—lived only a short time after his birth. Because the Lincolns did not own the land on which they lived, they buried baby Thomas in the Redmon family cemetery. In 1814, Thomas and Nancy sold their interest in their Mill Creek farm in Elizabethtown, possibly to pay court costs in the fight to regain the Sinking Spring farm.

Their misfortune continued. On December 27, 1815, they were served with an eviction from the Knob Creek farm Lincoln had leased from George Lindsey. It seemed the heirs of Thomas Middleton of Philadelphia, Pennsylvania, brought suit against the Lincolns, the Redmons, and nine other neighbors claiming that the Middletons were the rightful owners of the property. Again, Lincoln and his neighbors countered with their own legal action. Lindsey, Lincoln's landlord, hired and paid for the counsel representing his and Lincoln's rights to the property. However, Thomas Lincoln, named as a tenant in the eviction order, was again threatened with losing the family home.

On May 18, 1816, Thomas was appointed "surveyor of the road leading from Nolin to Bardstown," the turnpike that ran in front of their home. However, the appointment came barely four months after the unfavorable ruling on the Sinking Spring farm. That loss, plus the newer challenge to his tenure at Knob Creek, as well as the limited land for farming to feed his family, likely marked their decision to leave Kentucky. After living in the state for thirty-four years, Thomas Lincoln moved his family to Perry (now Spencer) County, Indiana, in December 1816, possibly drawn there by his brother Josiah's earlier move to Harrison County, Indiana. Ironically, not long after the move, the suit against the Knob Creek families was settled in their favor, but it was too little too late. By this time Thomas and Nancy, Abraham and Sarah had left Kentucky forever.

A full-page advertisement in Collier's *on February 25, 1906, solicited membership in the Lincoln Farm Association and emphasized endorsement by President Roosevelt who said: "Lincoln's memory, like Washington's, is one of the hallowed and priceless heritages of our people."*

To mark his birthplace

After Lincoln was assassinated in 1865, a Cincinnati publishing firm sent artist-journalist John B. Rowbotham to Hodgenville to take a photo of Lincoln's birthplace. Rowbotham found some rocks indicating the site of the cabin chimney on a little knoll or rise above the Sinking Spring, the first reference to the site following the Lincolns' move in 1811. By now the farm was owned by the Creal family, the Lincolns' former neighbors who claimed to remember Thomas Lincoln and his family.

Sadly, local and national efforts to commemorate Lincoln in Kentucky lagged behind endeavors undertaken by New York, Illinois, and Washington, D.C., because feelings toward Lincoln were mixed in his birth state, as they were with so many states because of the Civil War. But as the centennial of Abraham Lincoln's birth approached, interest in his life grew, especially from a few entrepreneurs. In 1894, Alfred W. Dennett, a New York-based businessman who planned to build a hotel and park on the historic spot, bought the Sinking Spring farm from Richard Creal. Dennett also purchased a cabin from John Davenport, who lived about a mile from the Sinking Spring farm,

"...this man, in whose heart knowledge and charity had left no room for malice, was marked by Providence as the one to 'bind up the Nation's wounds.' His birthplace is worth saving."

—Mark Twain, *New York Times,* January 13, 1907

27

The opening of the Lincoln Birthplace Memorial coincided with changing transportation patterns throughout the country. By 1930, Congressional appropriations extended the rock asphalt approach road from the park entrance on the Jackson Highway to a wide parking facility facing the Memorial Building. Each year more than eight thousand cars and countless bus tours visited the site, which cried out for supporting services. In 1928, James Richard Howell *(right)* opened the Nancy Lincoln Inn, named in honor of Lincoln's mother, to accommodate these visitors. Howell, a descendant of Kentucky pioneers whose sister Hattie Howell Howard purchased and began preserving the Knob Creek farm, was a prominent citizen in the community. He constructed the inn and four guest cabins from large chestnut logs, with the 16-by-18-foot, one-room cabins styled after what the Lincoln cabin might have resembled. The inn, contiguous to the birthplace historic site, provided a restaurant, museum, and gift shop in addition to the cabins. Still managed by the Howell family, the Nancy Lincoln Inn quickly became and remains a park partner in telling the Lincoln family story.

and erected it near the Sinking Spring in November 1895. His action would set in motion a myth that would persist for well over a century.

Lincoln Farm Association

On April 18, 1906, the Lincoln Farm Association was incorporated. Twenty-one individuals, including Richard Lloyd Jones, an editor for *Collier's Weekly*, agreed to raise money by voluntary subscription for the purpose of honoring and perpetuating the memory of Abraham Lincoln, developing the birthplace farm, and erecting monuments in Lincoln's honor. Years later, when asked to provide a history of the Lincoln Farm Association in 1940, Jones explained in a letter to the National Park Service regional director that his interest in Lincoln was inherited from his father. He was enticed by Colonel Henry Watterson, owner and editor of the Louisville *Courier Journal*, to visit the place of Lincoln's birth in Hodgenville. It was after this pivotal visit that Jones conceived the idea to build a memorial to Lincoln and convinced his employer, magazine publisher Robert J. Collier, to split the cost Jones paid at auction for the Sinking Spring farm.

Between 1906 and 1909, the Lincoln Farm Association raised over $400,000. To encourage the notion of "popular subscription," the association wrote in a letter to potential subscribers "that these funds shall be contributed, not by a wealthy few, but by the citizens of every state in the Union." Contributions from 25 cents to $25 entitled the contributor to an engraved membership certificate. Donations poured in but most came in twenty-five cent pieces, so they lifted the subscription amount. Association member Richard Lloyd Jones related that it took a corps of office workers such as those pictured here to handle the subscriptions and send out the certificates of appreciation for contributions.

29

The sale of the farm in 1906 attracted a great deal of attention. Newspapers called it a "sale of national importance . . .." Some 1,100 daily newspapers promised to run a series of articles on the fund-raising campaign. Robert Collier used his magazine to promote the newly formed Lincoln Farm Association and encourage contributions toward restoring the cabin and building a monument. President Theodore Roosevelt, himself devoted to Lincoln, stressed the importance of carrying out the improvements.

The Memorial Building

Momentum built in 1909 as the centennial of Lincoln's birth approached. Architect John Russell Pope was selected to design the Memorial Building that would house the cabin purported to be Lincoln's birthplace. Intending the birthplace to be the country's principle monument to Lincoln, the association envisioned a grand, two-story museum with an avenue of trees leading to the entrance. Granite from Milford, Massachusetts, clad the building's exterior, while the interior marble was quarried in Tennessee. Both states were sources for the pink stone popular in the era.

Pope's plans provided a dramatic approach: a wide formal stair of fifty-six steps, one for each year of Lincoln's life. Past the six-column Doric portico visitors would encounter two bronze-paneled doors with matching double doors at the north entrance. The original design also called for a copy of Augustus Saint-Gaudens' famous Lincoln statue, along with the celebrated cabin, to grace the central court that would feature a "removal" roof as described by the architect.

The soon-to-be celebrated architect John Russell Pope designed the Memorial Building early in his career. He would also design the Jefferson Memorial, the National Archives, and the National Gallery of Art. His first design for the Memorial Building, shown here, proved too costly, so it was simplified. Even so, the Memorial Building would become the first national memorial built to honor Abraham Lincoln's legacy.

However, funds fell short of the anticipated goal, and Pope's original plans were simplified.

Lincoln Birthday Centennial

A cold rain fell on February 12, 1909, the centennial of Lincoln's birth, but that did not deter President Theodore Roosevelt who, along with other notables of the time, slogged up the rain-soaked hill to deliver, in his characteristic style, a roaring tribute to his hero, Abraham Lincoln, and dedicate the cornerstone of the Memorial Building. The building was completed in 1910, and the association—satisfied (albeit mistakenly) by their investigation that they had the logs from Lincoln's birthplace cabin—enshrined it in the Memorial Building. One year later, in 1911, President William Howard Taft addressed a crowd of 3,000 during the Memorial Building's opening ceremonies.

The centennial of Lincoln's birth was celebrated around the country. Speeches, formal dinners, and fireworks marked the celebration from New York to San Francisco. Booklets containing Lincoln's most famous speeches were printed and centennial coins were issued. Those honoring Lincoln proudly wore ribbons and medals made for the occasion at county, state and national celebrations across the nation. President Roosevelt spoke at the birthplace of

Theodore Roosevelt so admired Lincoln that on his little finger he wore a "mourning ring" with a strand of Lincoln's hair during Roosevelt's presidential inauguration in 1905. This inkwell featuring the miniature bust of Lincoln was presented to Roosevelt when he was governor of New York, and he kept it on his desk in the library of his home (above left).

31

President Theodore Roosevelt and other distinguished guests prepare to lay the cornerstone of the Memorial Building February 12, 1909, the 100th anniversary of Abraham Lincoln's birth. The cornerstone for the Memorial Building is shown here just before it was laid that day. The vintage cabin photo shows what is believed to be Edith or Ethel Roosevelt taking a look inside the cabin during the cornerstone ceremony. Flyers, coins, pins and banners commemorated the date. The coins, each larger than a silver dollar, were distributed by the thousands. Roosevelt's remarks that day still resonate: "Excepting only Washington, Lincoln's figure stands foremost in all our history."

President William Howard Taft, a member of the Lincoln Farm Association, arrives to dedicate the Memorial Building on November 9, 1911. President Woodrow Wilson would be the third president to visit the site when, in 1916, he accepted the Sinking Spring farm as part of the National Park System.

Lincoln. Vice President Charles Fairbanks fulfilled the role of chief speaker in Harrisburg, Pennsylvania. In Springfield, Illinois, Robert Todd Lincoln, Abraham and Mary's firstborn son, listened to speeches delivered by William Jennings Bryan and the British and French ambassadors.

Birthplace receives National Park status

In 1911, the Lincoln Farm Association, their task complete, turned the park over to the state of Kentucky. One year later, in 1912, Congress considered the first two bills to convey the park to the federal government. But it was not until 1916, when President Woodrow Wilson signed the bill into law, that the Sinking Spring farm became federal property. Wilson traveled to the park to deliver an acceptance speech, the third visit by a president of the United States to Lincoln's place of birth. The War Department managed the site first under the direction of Richard Lloyd Jones who was appointed commissioner. Jurisdiction over the Abraham Lincoln Birthplace transferred from the War Department to the Department of the Interior in August 1933, thus preserving it as a national park.

Opposite: *Kentucky native redbud and dogwood trees, first planted during the War Department's administration of the site, frame the boundaries, adding glorious color to the landscape each spring.*

Part 2

Lincoln in Indiana

Making a New Home

By Mike Capps, Chief of Interpretation,
Lincoln Boyhood National Memorial

"My father . . . removed from Kentucky to what is now Spencer County, Indiana, in my eighth year. . . . There I grew up."

—A. Lincoln

Preceding pages: *When the Lincolns moved into southern Indiana in the early nineteenth century, they found it "covered with heavy timber," as Lincoln would later recall. It was a land of boundless opportunities but also of endless challenges. The task of clearing the land, as captured in this image by an unknown artist, was difficult, and many pioneers worked at it for years.*

This detail (left) of one of the five carved panels connecting the memorial cloister depicts family, friends, and various symbols of Lincoln's fourteen formative years in Indiana.

In the years following the War of 1812, emigration to the Old Northwest, which included Indiana, increased dramatically. With the defeat and relocation of the Indians, vast new acreage was opened to settlement. Large numbers of people from other parts of the country, many from Virginia, North Carolina, Tennessee, and Kentucky, began to move in. One such pioneer was Thomas Lincoln, who was attracted to Indiana by the rich land and the security of the systematic federal land survey, as stipulated in the Land Ordinance of 1785, as well as the absence of slavery.

Upon his return from a scouting trip to this new land in Indiana, Thomas and his family gathered their possessions and headed for the Ohio River crossing. It was December 1816—early winter—and Abraham was seven. He later remembered the trip to the farm site as one of the hardest experiences of his life. It took two weeks on unpaved roads and often through fields and woods to travel by horse-drawn wagon the one hundred miles from Kentucky to their new home in present-day Spencer County. They crossed the Ohio River at Thompson's ferry and followed an old wagon road for twelve miles. They hacked out the final distance through dense underbrush.

The trip west was only the beginning of their new adventure. When the Lincolns moved into southern Indiana in these early years of the 1800s, they found it "covered with heavy timber . . . three to four feet in diameter with trunks fifty to sixty feet high . . . ." It was a land of boundless opportunities but also of endless challenges. The immediate priority was shelter.

The forest's yield

At the first opportunity, Thomas began constructing a permanent home in the middle of this frontier. With the help of neighbors, Thomas cleared a spot on high ground and put up a log cabin on his 160-acre claim near the Little Pigeon Creek. Given the extensive surrounding forests, the log cabin was a natural choice for their dwellings. The early pioneers felled trees,

39

Lincoln Boyhood National Memorial

Just after Lincoln's assassination in 1865, artist John B. Rowbotham captured this image of a cabin supposed to have been built by Thomas Lincoln for his family in their new home in Indiana in 1829. Lincoln Boyhood National Memorial preserves the site of the farm in Lincoln City, Indiana, where Abraham Lincoln and his family lived from 1816 to 1830. It is a fitting tribute to the Lincoln family and Lincoln's time in Indiana, where he spent fourteen of his most formative years, from the age of seven to twenty-one. Today a graceful cloister connects the two formal memorial halls that make up the Memorial Building. Skilled stone masons carved in bas-relief various scenes from Lincoln's storied life. The museum in the Memorial Visitor Center details through exhibits Lincoln's frontier life here and how that period shaped him. The site also features the Nancy Hanks Lincoln gravesite and the Lincoln Living Historical Farm. Various trails link Lincoln's past to the present and lead visitors on a journey from the memorial to the Nancy Hanks Lincoln gravesite, the bronze Cabin Site Memorial and the Lincoln Living Historical Farm.

The Lincoln Boyhood National Memorial is located on Indiana Highway 162, between Dale to the north and Gentryville to the south.

often tulip poplar, about a foot in diameter, cut them to proper size and notched the ends so that corners would be level and secure. They cut doors and windows into the walls and added a fireplace and chimney at one end. Clay and mud filled the chinks between the logs, and a roof of wooden shingles topped the whole. Most cabins began with dirt floors; wooden floors were an addition that could wait until later.

The interior of the cabin was generally sparsely furnished with beds, stools, tables, chairs, and cupboards made by the settler out of the same trees that he cut to clear his land. He also fashioned utensils and serving dishes from wood or other natural materials such as gourds. They cooked over an open fire using a few items of iron cookware, such as a three-legged spider skillet or kettle.

In addition to raw materials for construction, the thick woods also provided an abundance of wild fruit, nuts, herbs, and berries, as well as a variety of wild game such as panthers, black bears, wolves, raccoons, white-tailed deer, woodland buffalo, wild turkeys and passenger pigeons. In fact, the Little Pigeon Creek community got its name from the vast flocks of passenger pigeons that used to blacken the sky.

The pioneers also had to make their own clothing, fashioning deerskin into moccasins, shirts and breeches. Women and girls also stayed constantly busy combing, carding, and spinning wool yarn and linen thread from the flax plant to produce "linsey-woolsey," a hard-wearing, coarse cloth used to make clothing. Nancy's skills as a seamstress were a blessing to the hard-working family.

Another challenge these frontier farmers faced was clearing the forested land for crops. The Lincoln family lived on wild game and bartered corn and pork that first winter, until Thomas could clear enough ground for his first crop. For this, he used the felling axe, a tool that had been in existence for centuries, but modified by the American pioneer for the unique conditions of the frontier. The addition of a heavy poll on the head opposite the blade added weight that made it more effective when swung to chop down a tree.

Young Lincoln, the rail splitter

Young Lincoln was large for his age, and his father put a felling ax into his hands at once. He became especially skilled in its use. One of his companions stated, "If you heard him felling trees in a clearing, you would say there were three men at work." In later life Abraham himself described how he "...was almost constantly handling that most useful instrument…" to combat the "…trees and bogs and grubs…" of the "unbroken wilderness" that was Indiana in the early nineteenth century. Another reality of pioneer life also left a deep impression, as he would later recall. A few days before Abraham's eighth birthday, a flock of wild turkeys approached the cabin. Standing inside, he fired his father's rifle through a crack in the cabin wall and shot one. He wrote many years later in an autobiography, "He has never since pulled a trigger on any larger game."

This task of hand clearing the forest was arduous, and pioneers worked at it for years. According to one settler, the "first clearing was done in a 'hurry-up-and-get-in-a-crop' style." For larger trees they sometimes used the process of girdling, or the cutting of a ring through the bark of the tree. This cut the lifeline of the tree and led to its death. Walnut, hickory, elm, and beech never put out leaves again after being girdled while in full leaf, but hackberry and ash required deep burning. To dispatch these, the farmer piled underbrush and smaller cleared trees around them and set them ablaze. The following winter, the farmers either set fire to the dead trees still standing or simply left them until they fell on their own. Oak, poplar, and walnut would stand for several years.

One aspect of the timber-clearing process developed into an important social event. Once the trees had been chopped down, neighbors gathered together for the "log rolling" to tug the dead trees into piles for burning. The children played, and the women cooked, visited and spread the tables for dining. The men formed teams and, armed with handspikes—tough, seasoned saplings about six feet long and three inches wide that were driven into the logs—the teams proceeded to carry and drag the logs to the piles. An intense but usually good-natured rivalry determined the faster or stronger teams. The "rolling" usually concluded with a big dinner.

The fires from these great heaps of logs would burn for days, sending off a pungent, eye-stinging smoke that permeated the settlements and made work in the area impossible for a time. One Indiana pioneer later related his memories of log rolling in the 1820s: "It was a purty sight to see all them big piles of logs a burnin', especially at night. Such a poppin' and a crackin' and a shootin' of flames and sparks high in the air! The big fires would throw out so much light it would turn darkness into daylight. The heat and smoke would be so bad you couldn't go near for a day or so. When the fires did die down enough, we went in with our handspikes and righted the heaps by pryin' and pushin' the

It took the Lincoln family approximately two weeks to travel by wagon the one hundred miles from their home in Kentucky to their new home in Indiana. Today it takes about two-and-a-half hours to make the same trip by car.

"Labor is the great source from which nearly all, if not all, human comforts and necessities are drawn."

—A. Lincoln

Thomas Lincoln *(right)* was a hardworking man who was well respected in the community. In addition to managing the farm and looking after his family, he was a carpenter and skilled cabinetmaker. Most likely his son, Abraham, aided him. Both the pie safe and tools pictured here are attributed to Thomas Lincoln, according to Library of Congress records. Although there are no known photographs of Nancy Hanks Lincoln, this drawing *(lower left)* by Lloyd Ostendorf captures the young mother, described by her cousin John Hanks as 5 feet 7 inches in height, 120 pounds, with dark hair and hazel eyes. Like most pioneer women, she shared equally with her husband in the burdens of frontier life, including clothing the family in deerskin or rough fabric spun from the fibers of the blue-flowering flax plant that grew all around.

logs together so they would keep burnin'. Log heaps would burn and smolder for several days. In fact, there was nearly always a burnin' or smoldern' log heap around a settler's cabin when he was clearin' land. It was a good place to get live coals if the fire went out in the fireplace."

But clearing the land was only the first step to productive farming. Initially the farmer had to plow around tree stumps, which remained firmly in place for years. Only after they were old and dry could the stumps be burned out. Acre by acre, the backbreaking process of clearing started all over again on the next parcel of land. Father and son Lincoln worked side by side to clear the land, plant the crops and build a home. Wrote Benjamin P. Thomas, "Year by year the forest yielded grudgingly to their axes until they had planted some seventeen acres in corn, wheat and oats."

Thomas' skills as a carpenter were in demand as the community grew. In addition to managing a farm and providing for his family, his carpentry work brought in extra income. Most likely aided by his young son, Thomas also helped build the Little Pigeon Baptist Church, where he was a member and served as church trustee. By 1827, he had earned enough money to pay his debt on one hundred acres of land.

Lineage, loss, and a mother's love

Thomas Lincoln's reputation has suffered at the hands of many historians over the years. He has often been described as a ne'er-do-well, and it has been speculated that the relationship between him and his son Abraham was distant at best. Available evidence, however, suggests a more tempered view. By all contemporary accounts, Thomas Lincoln was a well-respected and responsible member of his community. An inventory of the property he sold when he decided to leave Indiana indicates that he had actually done quite well. As for the father-son relationship, two years after his father's death, Lincoln named one of his sons after him —Thomas (Tad) Lincoln born in 1853.

While Nancy's cousin Dennis Hanks recalled of young Abraham that Thomas would "sometimes knock him over," harsh frontier life did not allow for gentle discipline. A child's life often depended on a parent's swift, definitive scolding. Based on his own background, Thomas may have also found it difficult to embrace his son's passion for books and a life of the mind.

"I was raised to farm work, which I continued till I was twenty-two."

—A. Lincoln

Opposite: *An interpreter at the Lincoln Living Historical Farm goes about his chores much as Thomas Lincoln did in his lifetime.*

On the other hand, Dennis Hanks also described Thomas as "one of the best men that ever lived. A sturdy, honest, God fearing man whom all the neighbors respected." He was described as good-humored, patient, kind, and "loving everybody and everything." His friendly good nature was supplemented with a flair for storytelling. "He had a great stock of...anecdotes and professed a marvelous proclivity to entertain by 'spinning yarns'...."

This description of the father's personality fit Abraham as well. Stories of the son's honesty have become almost legendary; examples of his compassion and desire for "malice toward none" epitomize kindness and mercy; and his reputation for storytelling and humor are now synonymous with Abraham Lincoln. Thoughts of Lincoln instantly bring to mind his virtue and integrity. In the words of a fellow family member, "Abe got his honesty and his clean notions of living and kind heart from his father." Though difficult to assess, Thomas undoubtedly made many intangible contributions to the development of Abraham's character. The influence of his father was deep and everlasting.

Despite the hard work, life was generally good for the Lincolns during their first two years in Indiana. They soon had the company of family nearby as well, for Thomas and Elizabeth Sparrow, Nancy's uncle and aunt who had raised her from childhood, had also migrated to Indiana in the fall of 1817. They brought with them their nephew and Nancy's eighteen-year-old cousin, Dennis Hanks, who slept in the loft with Abraham and became his companion and playmate despite their difference in age.

As it did so often with pioneer families, tragedy soon struck. In October 1818, when Abraham was nine years old, his mother, Nancy Hanks Lincoln, died of the "milk sickness" at age thirty-four. The scourge of the frontier, milk sickness afflicted those who drank the contaminated milk or ate the meat of a cow infected with the toxin from the white snakeroot plant. Nancy had gone to nurse and comfort the Sparrows, who were now neighbors, and became herself a victim of the dreaded disease. With heavy hearts, Thomas and Abraham whipsawed logs into planks, and, with wooden pegs, they fastened the boards together into a coffin for the beloved wife and mother. She was buried on a wooded hill south of the cabin.

Her death was a tragic blow, the first of many tragedies her son would later face in life. By all accounts she had been a fine

Opposite: Abraham worked alongside his father, clearing land, planting and harvesting crops, and tending livestock. He became especially proficient with an axe, and many would later remark about his ability to fell trees and split them into rails for fences. In 1860, when he ran for president, Lincoln would be called "the rail splitter" candidate.

This stone, which once marked the site of the cabin a few hundred feet west of where Lincoln lived, is now part of the Trail of Twelve Stones at the Lincoln Boyhood National Memorial in Indiana.

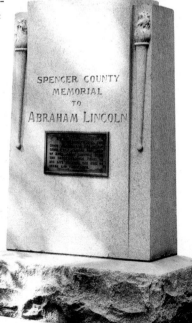

Love and Loss

It is impossible to assess the full impact of Nancy's life and death on Abraham Lincoln, but his reminiscences of her later in his life reflected deep love and loss. She died of milk sickness caused by drinking milk from a cow that had grazed on the white snakeroot plant *(pictured at right)* common in the area. A three-dimensional diorama at the Lincoln Boyhood Museum depicts her burial, while an unknown artist captured the grieving little family at the gravesite *(right)*. The loss of his sister Sarah in childbirth was another grief that would affect Abraham profoundly. She and her infant are buried in the gravesite in the cemetery of the Little Pigeon Baptist Church, the same church Thomas Lincoln helped to build not far from their homestead.

Left with two little ones and desperately needing a helpmate after Nancy's death, Thomas Lincoln remarried in 1819, to widow Sarah "Sally" Bush Johnston. Abraham remained close to his stepmother and always referred to her as "Mother."

"I view [education] as the most important subject which we as people can be engaged in."

—A. Lincoln

and loving mother who undoubtedly left her mark on the young boy in the countless small and intimate ways that mothers do. She had also been a guiding force in his life, encouraging him to read and explore the world through books. His memory of her was still strong some forty years later when he said, "All that I am or ever hope to be I owe to her."

With young Sarah and Abraham now without a mother and Thomas without a wife, the family keenly felt Nancy's absence. In 1819, Thomas returned to Kentucky to seek the hand of Sarah Bush Johnston, a widow with three children. Having known Sarah before he moved to Indiana, and knowing she was now a widow, he paid her a visit and asked her to marry him. They were married on December 2, 1819, and Sarah and her three children—John, Matilda, and Elizabeth—returned with Thomas to Indiana, where Sarah, known as Sally, set about merging the two families. She found the country to be "wild and desolate" but the log cabin that Thomas had built was "good, tolerably comfortable."

Sarah saw right away her new stepson's intelligence and his passion for knowledge; he was especially fond of reading. Her gift to him of three books—*The Arabian Nights, Webster's Speller,* and *Robinson Crusoe*—left an indelible impression on him and was a priceless treasure on a frontier where books were scarce. It also reassured him that, like his mother, Sarah encouraged his quest for learning. The two quickly developed a close, intimate, mother-son relationship that would continue for the rest of Abraham's life. Lincoln said of his stepmother "she proved to be a good and kind mother" to him. By all reports their relationship was excellent, and Mrs. Lincoln considered her stepson a model child who was always honest, witty, and "diligent for knowledge." He never needed a "cross word," as she recalled.

After the family moved to Illinois and Abraham had gone out on his own, he still found time to visit. Sally Lincoln reported that she "saw him every year or two," the last time when he visited to bid her farewell before going to Washington for his inauguration. When she later recalled the visit after her stepson's death in 1865, she wept. Sarah died in 1869.

For want of an education

The demands of life on the frontier left little time for young Abraham to attend school. "The aggregate of all his schooling did not amount to one year. He was never in a college or academy as a student. What he has

A Life of the Mind

Despite limited schooling, Lincoln's fertile mind kept him studying on his own, and he devoured books. For Abraham, to get books and read them "...was the main thing." One of his favorites was *Aesop's Fables*, from which he liked reciting stories to his friends. He also enjoyed adventure tales like *Pilgrim's Progress* and *Ivanhoe* and would read the books he liked over and over again. He considered the Bible "the best gift God has given to man" and quoted it often. He even read Indiana law books and court proceedings. Fascinated by the lives of Washington and Franklin, he studied the *Life of Washington* written by Mason Weems as well as the pages of Benjamin Franklin's *Autobiography*. Both were clearly the sources of some of his ideas about patriotism and government. Lincoln would later say, "I recollect thinking then, boy though I was, that there must have been something more than common that these men struggled for." Artist E. Johnson captured young

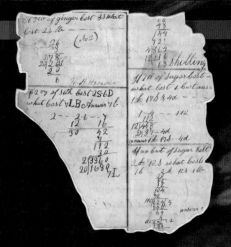

Lincoln reading by fireplace light in this 1868 lithograph. On display at the Lincoln Boyhood site are copies of some of the books he read and pages from the copybook in which he worked math problems and wrote lines of verse, practicing the careful penmanship that would one day become so widely recognized.

In Remembrance

Interest in Nancy Hanks Lincoln's gravesite is significant because it represents that period within the history of the preservation movement when the creation of memorial edifices and landscapes was an important expression of the nation's respect and reverence for Abraham Lincoln. In this sketch *(below)* by John B. Rowbotham in the 1860s, he depicts himself being shown the location of Nancy's neglected gravesite by what appears to be a young boy. Civil War veteran William Q. Corbin visited the site and lamented its condition in a verse he published in the Rockport *Journal* in November 1868:

*A wooded hill – a low sunk grave
Upon a hilltop hoary;
The Oak tree's branches o'er it wave;
Devoid of slab – no record save
Tradition's story*

This first public account eventually prompted several Gentryville businessmen to meet on December 24, 1869, to discuss erecting a suitable marker. It would take another decade before an 1879 newspaper article reporting the neglect prompted Peter E. Studebaker, second vice president of the Studebaker Carriage Company, to contact Rockport postmaster L.S. Gilkey with instructions

to buy the best tombstone available for $50 and place it anonymously on the site. Another $50, solicited from area residents, paid for an elegant iron fence around the grave *(inset)* that set Nancy's grave apart from others. Finally, in 1909, the state took over and cleared the park of dead trees, built a road to the gravesite and erected a fence with an elaborate entrance gate *(far left)*. The highway entrance featured life-sized lions, while eagles perched on columns closer to the gravesite. Large stone urns lined the roadway to Nancy's final resting place. Both the gate and fence were later removed. Only the simple headstone remains today.

In April 1865, just days after Lincoln's assassination, some residents of the nearby town of Elizabeth (later to be known as Dale) went to the Lincoln farm area and posed for pictures in front of what was reputed to be the 1829 cabin *(lower right)*. But efforts to preserve Lincoln's Indiana home site would evolve throughout the late nineteenth and early twentieth centuries, finally culminating in the establishment of the Nancy Hanks Lincoln Memorial Park in 1926. That same year, the Indiana Lincoln Union began its campaign to raise funds for development of the park. They hired a New York advertising firm to handle newspaper publicity, and more than 200,000 letters were sent to Indiana citizens and institutions soliciting support for the memorial. Their ad *(left)* included a drawing of the cabin "made in 1869 while the cabin was still standing," and cited a score of reasons why

Indiana must build a memorial in tribute to their famous "Hoosier." On July 12, 1932, dignitaries and supporters formally dedicated a towering 120-foot flagpole in an island in the center of the plaza. Pictured above is the Memorial Plaza around 1934, prior to construction of the Memorial Building.

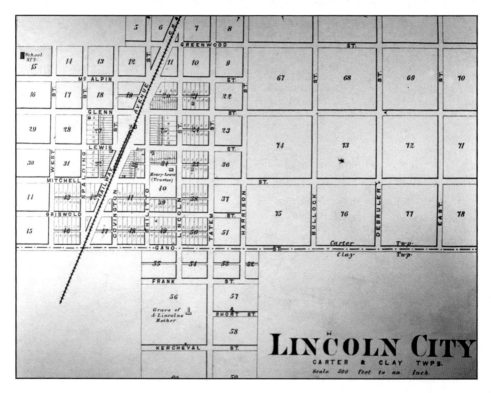

This map is based on the original plat done in 1872 for Lincoln City, a stop on the railroad line running diagonally at left. Named for the statesman who literally put it on the map, it was predicted to become a big city. It did grow rapidly at first, due to the railroad, farming goods and local coal mines. At one point, passenger trains made twelve round trips a day to area cities. But the boom did not last. Although the railroad still operates a freight line through the "city," the town is nearly all residential. Its name is fitting, since it remains the destination for thousands of tourists who make the pilgrimage every year to see where Abraham Lincoln was raised and educated.

in the way of education he has picked up. After he was twenty-three and he had separated from his father, he studied English grammar—imperfectly of course, but so as to speak and write as well as he now does. He regrets his want of education and does what he can to supply the want." So wrote Abraham Lincoln on the subject of his education in a third-person autobiography written after he began public life.

It was an education acquired, as he put it, "by littles." Schooling opportunities were scarce in these frontier times, since few people were literate enough to teach. Referring to his educational opportunities in Indiana, Abraham stated, "There were schools, so called, but little qualification was ever required of a teacher. If a straggler supposed to understand Latin happened to sojourn in the neighborhood, he was looked upon as a wizard. There was absolutely nothing to excite ambition for education. When I came of age I did not know much. Still somehow, I could read, write, and cipher to the Rule of Three; but that was all."

But education was something Thomas and Nancy Lincoln, and later Sarah Lincoln, wanted for their children, so they sent them to whatever school was available. Lincoln attended terms of school mostly in the winter when outdoor work was less pressing. He even recalled the names of his five teachers. In his eleventh

Carved in Stone

The designers and builders of the Memorial Building made every effort to choose building materials and to use construction methods that would evoke the pioneer era. Native tulip poplar trusses were finished by hand using broad axes and adzes. Local residents hired to do the work hand hewed the timbers. Five limestone panels weighing 10 tons and measuring 8 feet tall by 13 1/2 feet wide were quarried. The sculptor, Elmer H. Daniels, is shown below personally inspecting one of the slabs at the quarry. In another image, he pauses from work on one of the clay models that would be used to create the sculpted panels that are an integral part of the memorial. As part of the plan for the cloister of the memorial, architect Richard Bishop included five sculptured panels separated by four large openings. The

panels represent Lincoln's life in Kentucky, Indiana, Illinois, and Washington, with the fifth representing the deceased president's significance to all Americans. Passages from his speeches cut into the stone and doorways echo across the top of the memorial.

year, he studied under Andrew Crawford, a stern, yet capable, teacher. Crawford loaned Abraham a copy of Mason Weems' *Life of Washington*, a book that profoundly influenced the young student. During his fourteenth year, Abraham briefly attended the school taught by James Swaney. Later, at the age of seventeen, Lincoln attended school under the tutelage of Azel W. Dorsey. Under him, Abraham probably received his best instruction, for Dorsey was the best educated and well trained of Lincoln's Indiana teachers and probably was responsible for helping him acquire his excellent grasp of mathematics. Years later, Dorsey could still remember the boy as "marked for the diligence and eagerness with which he pursued his studies, [he] came to the log cabin schoolhouse arrayed in buck skin clothes, a raccoon-skin cap, and provided with an old arithmetic."

Opposite and above: The interior furnishings for the Indiana memorial's internal spaces, including the cherry table, chairs, benches, and the pews in the Abraham Lincoln Hall, were custom made by local artisans from wood acquired especially for the project.

Fledgling entrepreneur, orator and litigator

Lincoln's growing-up years in Indiana were full of challenges, for his body as well as his mind. He continued to grow and, by the time he was a teenager, he stood six-foot-four. He could wrestle with the best, and local people remembered that he could lift more weight and drive an axe deeper than any man around. When

This Lloyd Ostendorf drawing depicts young Lincoln resting from his chores, engaging in his favorite pastime—reading.

Trail of Twelve Stones

As construction of the Memorial Building progressed, workers made modifications to the surrounding landscape. Teams of horses were used to reshape the area around the Memorial Building, as seen in this photo *(far right)* taken around 1940. Workers with the Civilian Conservation Corps planted nearly 40,000 native trees and shrubs. A small flower garden planted near the service area provided flowers for Nancy Lincoln's grave. As far back as 1931, the Indiana Lincoln Union began planning the "Trail of Twelve Stones" as part of the boyhood site, to commemorate the "stepping stones" in Lincoln's life and career. The stones found along the one-mile winding trail include a rock from a spring near Abraham Lincoln's birthplace at Hodgenville, Kentucky; a rock *(right)* from the store at Jonesboro, Indiana, where he worked as a clerk; a stone from the cottage where Lincoln wrote the Emancipation Proclamation; a boulder from Gettysburg; and a portion of a column at the house where Lincoln died.

THIS ROCK WAS PART
OF THE JONES STORE AT
JONESBORO, 3 MILES WEST
OF HERE, ASSOCIATED WITH
LINCOLN'S EARLY MANHOOD.

INDIANA LINCOLN UNION

Dedication of the Monument in memory of Nancy Hanks Lincoln, Mother of the Martyred President, erected at her grave, near Lincoln City, Spencer County, Indiana, through the generosity of Mr. J. S. Culver, of Springfield, Illinois, under the auspices of the Indiana Nancy Hanks Lincoln Memorial Association

J. S Culver had the contract for remodeling the Lincoln tomb in Springfield, Illinois, and he offered to recut one of the discarded stones from that memorial and present it to the Nancy Hanks Lincoln Memorial Association for her gravesite. They accepted the offer and dedicated the large Culver stone (above right) in October 1902. Fifteen thousand people were reported to have attended the ceremony. The Culver stone was later moved and became part of the Trail of Twelve Stones, one of three trails that guide the visitor to the various historic areas within the park site.

his father could spare him, he sometimes earned extra money – some 25 cents a day – doing chores on neighboring farms. He also worked as a helper for James Taylor, who operated a ferry across the mouth of the Anderson River. In his spare time he built a scow to take passengers out to the steamers on the Ohio. As described by biographer Benjamin Thomas, "One day two travelers rushed down to the riverbank, crying for transportation to a steamboat lying off the creek-mouth. Sculling his cumbersome scow . . . , young Lincoln brought them alongside the steamer just as it took off, and as the two men clambered aboard, he pitched their carpetbags after them." To his surprise, each threw him a silver half-dollar. "I could scarcely credit that I, a poor boy, had earned a dollar in less than a day," he would later relate.

Although profitable, his business venture also led to one of his first encounters with the legal system. Two brothers who held the ferry rights across the Ohio between Kentucky and Indiana charged Lincoln with encroaching on their jurisdiction. Kentucky law, in such cases, provided for the violator to be fined. But the judge dismissed the charge, ruling that, because Lincoln did not carry his passengers all the way across

Historic Hearthstones

While working on the extensive landscaping for the memorial in May 1933, the Civilian Conservation Corps crew located the historic hearthstones of the original cabin. They were situated in a T-configuration and comprised three layers of stones measuring roughly eighteen inches square and five to six inches deep. The crew, under the supervision of Site Superintendent Horace Weber, uncovered the 300 hearthstones, constructed a stone wall around the site and landscaped the grounds. In the photo below, Weber examines the hearthstones. Today a bronze memorial designed by Thomas Hibben marks the site of the 1829 cabin. Cast from an actual cabin foundation, the memorial symbolizes the home the Lincolns occupied during their Indiana years.

Newspaper articles in the 1960s advocated creation of a national park at Lincoln's boyhood home.

the river but only to the steamboats, he had not violated the law.

In 1828, James Gentry, the richest man in the community, hired Lincoln to accompany Gentry's son Allen to New Orleans in a flatboat loaded with produce. The thousand-mile journey would take three months, exposing nineteen-year-old Lincoln to a bustling city and a whole new way of life. While in New Orleans, he witnessed a slave auction on the docks. As Allen Gentry would later recall, it was a sight that greatly disturbed Lincoln and made a strong and lasting impression.

After their return by steamboat, Abraham continued to work intermittently for Gentry at his store. He also began to take an interest in politics. The Gentry store was often a gathering place for local residents and where Abraham listened as a number of political views were aired. At home there was more talk of politics, and he began to form his own opinions. With his keen mind and gift for language, he was able to make his own contributions to the lively discussions.

Abraham also developed his talent for public speaking during this time. One of the books his stepmother gave him was *Lessons in Elocution*, which contained famous speeches, passages from literature, and rules for improving oratory skills that likely informed the young orator. Legend has it that he practiced making speeches standing on a tree stump and imitating the style of preachers and politicians. He became well known for his dry wit, simple language, and brevity. Yet later in life Lincoln would say that he was uncomfortable speaking unless he had something to say.

Another loss, another journey

The same year of his steamboat journey, Abraham experienced another devastating loss. His sister Sarah Lincoln was an important person in Abraham Lincoln's life, and they had always shared a close relationship. While the family was still living in Kentucky, she had taken Abraham with her when she had started school and had probably helped him learn his letters and numbers. When their mother died, the siblings comforted each other in their grief. Their relationship was characterized by a deep affection. As a neighbor said, "They were close companions and were a great deal alike in temperament." Sarah's kind and loving care of him likely influenced Abraham's development of these same traits.

A description of Sarah comes from her stepmother who described her as "short of stature and somewhat

plump in build, her hair was dark brown and her eyes were gray." Her brother-in-law Nathaniel Grigsby would later describe Sarah as "a woman of extraordinary mind. Her good-humored laugh I can hear now, is as fresh in my mind as if it were yesterday. She could, like her brother, meet and greet a person with the kindest greeting in the world, make you easy at the touch of a word, an intellectual and intelligent woman."

On August 2, 1826, Sarah married Aaron Grigsby, and the new couple moved into a cabin two miles south of the Lincolns. Nine months after their marriage, Sarah announced to her family that she was pregnant. But complications during the delivery claimed both her life and that of her infant child. A neighbor recalled: "I remember the night she died. My mother was there at the time. She had a strong voice, and I heard her calling her father. He went after a doctor, but it was too late. They let her lay too long." Sarah died January 20, 1828, at the age of twenty-one.

President John F. Kennedy signed the act authorizing the establishment of Lincoln Boyhood National Memorial on February 19, 1962, the first unit of the National Park System in Indiana.

One more move

By all accounts, the Lincolns prospered in Indiana, but in 1830 Thomas decided to move once again, this time to Illinois, where Sarah Bush Lincoln's relatives described the soil as rich and productive. Milk sickness, which once again threatened the Little Pigeon community and had claimed Nancy, did not exist there. Thomas sold his property, and the extended Lincoln family piled all their goods into three wagons, one drawn by horses, the other two by oxen, and headed for the land of promise. They pulled slowly away from the homestead, picked up the road to Vincennes about four miles north, and plodded steadily toward Illinois. It was March 1, 1830. Atop one of the ox-drawn wagons sat Abraham Lincoln, just turned twenty-one. On March 6, the caravan crossed the Wabash, flooded by spring rains. Within the month they came at last to John Hanks' place on the north bank of the Sangamon River, eight miles west of Decatur, Illinois. Abraham Lincoln, product of the Kentucky hills and Indiana forests, had reached the prairie country that would claim his next thirty years. Initially he would settle with his family in Macon County, but by now he was a young man who would soon strike out on his own.

Lincoln Boyhood National Memorial

After the Lincolns left Illinois in 1830, the land that Thomas owned was sold several times and subdivided. Others occupied the cabin he had started in 1829. Although no traces of the Lincoln cabin could be found, in 1917 Spencer County placed a marker on the reputed 1829 site. Following Abraham Lincoln's death in 1865, interest in his Indiana homesite was revived, and a series of visitors would set in motion its eventual preservation.

In September 1865, just five months after Lincoln's assassination, his Springfield law partner, William Herndon, visited the farm site and talked with local residents as he gathered information for his biography of the late president. He was followed by John B. Rowbotham (the same artist dispatched to Sinking Spring farm), who made a drawing of what was purported to be the Lincoln cabin. In 1868, a Civil War veteran named William Q. Corbin visited the boyhood home of his former commander-in-chief. His poem lamenting the neglected burial site of the mother of the president would be the first known public account of the grave's condition. Despite this interest, it was 1879 before a newspaper article reporting the neglect prompted Peter E. Studebaker, second vice president of the Studebaker Carriage Company, to contact Rockport postmaster L.S. Gilkey with instructions to buy the best tombstone available for $50 and place it anonymously on the site. Another $50, solicited from area residents, paid for an iron fence around the grave.

Headstones, hearthstones, a new city and a new union

At the same time this stone was being acquired and prepared, several Cincinnati, Ohio, businessmen were developing what remained of the Little Pigeon community into what became known as Lincoln City, a stop along the railroad line they were building. This community was to have a great impact on the Lincoln boyhood home site. Fortunately, a local resident convinced the developers to donate the half-acre surrounding the gravesite to Spencer County. In June 1880, a ten-man commission was organized to maintain the site, but their efforts proved sporadic. By the 1890s, it was reported that the site was again in poor condition, and in 1909 the state took possession of the gravesite.

The Trail of Twelve Stones at the Boyhood site includes this rock from the area where Lincoln stood when he delivered the Gettysburg Address.

Indiana celebrated its centennial in December 1916. Among the centennial programs was a thrust to identify locations important to the state's history. In 1917, Spencer County's centennial commission, with the assistance of older residents of the county, determined the approximate location of Thomas Lincoln's cabin, and interest in the historic Lincoln property increased.

In 1926, a group of private citizens formed the Indiana Lincoln Union to coordinate the work of the various patriotic organizations that had shown an interest in the project. One of the ILU's first recommendations was that the state hire noted landscape architect Frederick Law Olmsted Jr. to prepare preliminary designs for a memorial.

Olmsted visited Lincoln City in March 1927 to review the site and came back in May to present his ideas. He conceived of a memorial of strength, sentiment and reason, yet simple, so as not to overwhelm the "familiar associations" of the area with the Lincolns. But neither did he want to merely restore the area to its natural condition. He wanted to create a formal memorial landscape with an allee (a formal lane lined with trees or other landscaping) that extended from a plaza to the south of the gravesite up toward the wooded knoll where Nancy Hanks Lincoln was buried. The state and the ILU embraced his ideas enthusiastically, and fund-raising enabled the state to acquire and begin developing additional property.

In 1933, the state budgeted money for a bronze memorial to be placed at the historic cabin site and for construction of the "Trail of Twelve Stones"

The Lincoln Living Historical Farm, a re-creation of a pioneer farm, gives visitors a vivid picture of life as Lincoln lived it. Fully furnished structures, including the 22-by-16-foot cabin, smokehouse, corn crib, carpenter shop, and barn, provide a historic backdrop for park interpreters in 1820s period clothing who perform a variety of pioneer tasks. Nearby fields are cultivated using historic varieties of crops and methods of farming.

commemorating various aspects of Abraham Lincoln's life. After deciding that it would be inappropriate to construct a replica of the Lincoln cabin, the state hired architect Thomas Hibben, a native of Indiana, to design a suitable monument to mark the site that would feature a bronze casting in the shape of the historic cabin sill and hearth, to be surrounded by a stone wall, with formal landscaping around the area. The ILU ultimately subcontracted the project to a company in Munich, Germany. After numerous delays in shipment due to political unrest in Germany, the bronze casting was finally received and placed on the site in July 1935, one of the more notable achievements in the effort to memorialize the Lincoln site.

Lincoln Boyhood Memorial Building

Placement of the casting marked completion of the first phase of the memorial's development, and the state moved on to the second: that of constructing a memorial building. In an effort to keep the structure simple, architect Richard Bishop (who partnered with landscape architect Olmsted in the overall design) analyzed the functional requirements and identified three basic needs: a central memorial feature, a small hall suitable for public meetings, and a large room with simple facilities for the comfort of visitors. He translated these needs into the three architectural units of the building: the central memorial court, the Abraham Lincoln Hall, and the less formal Nancy Hanks Lincoln Hall, which included restroom facilities.

As part of the plan for the cloister, Bishop included five sculptured panels separated by four large openings. The panels would represent Lincoln's life in Kentucky, Indiana, Illinois, and Washington, with the fifth representing the deceased president's significance to all Americans. Passages from Lincoln's speeches would be carved in stone above the panels and the doorways.

Bishop designed the memorial to employ as completely as possible Indiana materials that would have been available in the early nineteenth century. The ILU awarded contracts for construction in late 1940. The hand-cut limestone for the panels came from Bloomington, Indiana; the Department of Conservation furnished the native timbers and finished lumber; and the cherry table, chairs, benches, and the pews in the Abraham Lincoln Hall were custom made by local artisans from wood acquired especially for the project.

Work on the sculptured panels was delayed until 1941 when the ILU finally hired Indiana sculptor Elmer H. Daniels. Daniels set up a studio in Jasper in September of that year and began preparing pencil sketches. He then created 16-by-27-inch clay models. Following oversight committee approval of the models, Daniels then prepared half-scale clay models of each panel from which plaster casts were made. Five limestone panels weighing 10 tons and measuring 8 feet tall by 13½ feet wide were quarried. Stone carvers hired by the Department of Conservation had completed the panels by the spring of 1942, just six months after Daniels had been brought onboard.

Coincident with construction of the Memorial Building, some modifications were also made to the surrounding landscape. Workers moved stone benches from the Cabin Site Memorial to the corners of the plaza; the flagpole was moved to the hill at the top of the allee in 1944; and grass and flowering shrubs filled the Memorial Courtyard.

The Lincoln Boyhood National Memorial features the tallest flagpole in Indiana. It measures 120 feet, 6 inches.

Boyhood site transfers to National Park Service

With completion of the Memorial Building, the development of the Nancy Hanks Lincoln Memorial was essentially complete. Life for the next twenty years was relatively quiet.

By the late 1950s, talk began of transferring the memorial to the federal government and making a national park of it. In 1959, Senator Vance Hartke of Evansville introduced a bill into Congress that authorized the National Park Service to conduct a feasibility study. Although the study did not recommend against it, neither did it endorse the idea. In the meantime, though, local businessman William Koch championed the idea and worked with Congressman Winfield K. Denton to introduce legislation proposing the establishment of a National Park Service unit at Lincoln City. With state endorsement and the offer to donate the two hundred acres containing the cabin site, the gravesite, and the Memorial Building, the legislation passed easily. President John F. Kennedy signed the act authorizing the establishment of the Lincoln Boyhood National Memorial on February 19, 1962. On July 10, 1962, in a ceremony in front of the Memorial Building, the transfer was formally made, and Indiana's first authorized unit of the National Park System was dedicated.

1782 — Abraham Lincoln senior sells Virginia farm and moves to Jefferson County, Kentucky

1784 — Nancy Hanks born in Virginia; later moves to Kentucky

1786 — Abraham senior killed by American Indian

1803 — Thomas Lincoln purchases Mill Creek farm in Elizabethtown

1806 — Nancy and Thomas Lincoln wed in Washington County (Springfield), Kentucky; move to Mill Creek farm

1807 — Sarah Lincoln born

1808 — Thomas Lincoln purchases Sinking Spring farm, thirteen miles from Elizabethtown near Hodgen's Mill

1809 — February 12, Abraham Lincoln born at Sinking Spring farm in Hardin (now LaRue) County, Kentucky

1811 — Lincoln family evicted from Sinking Spring farm; lease land in Knob Creek Valley

1814 — Thomas and Nancy Lincoln sell Mill Creek farm

1816 — Thomas Lincoln moves his family to Spencer County, Indiana

1818 — Nancy Hanks Lincoln dies

1819 — Thomas Lincoln marries Sarah Bush Johnston

1828 — Abraham Lincoln journeys to New Orleans by flatboat; witnesses slave auction; Sara Lincoln Grigsby dies in childbirth

1830 — Thomas Lincoln family moves to Illinois

1831 — Abraham Lincoln arrives in New Salem

1832 — Lincoln serves in Black Hawk War; loses first political race (for legislature)

1834 — Lincoln elected to state legislature; begins studying law

1836 — Re-elected to state legislature; receives law license

1837 — Lincoln delivers first public opinion against slavery; moves to Springfield; joins law partnership with John T. Stuart

1838	Re-elected to legislature	**1855**	Defeated for Senate
1840	Re-elected to legislature	**1856**	Joins Republican Party; finishes second in balloting for Republican vice presidential nomination; campaigns for Republican Party
1841	Forms law partnership with Stephen T. Logan		
1842	Marries Mary Todd	**1858**	Nominated for Senate by Republican convention; Lincoln-Douglas debates

		1859	Defeated for Senate
1843	Robert Todd Lincoln born	**1860**	Delivers Cooper Institute address; elected president; South Carolina secedes
1844	Lincolns purchase their Springfield home; Lincoln forms law partnership with William Herndon	**1861**	Lincoln departs Springfield for inauguration; Fort Sumter bombarded; Civil War begins with a total of 11 states seceding
		1862	Willie Lincoln dies
1846	Edward Baker (Eddie) Lincoln born; Abraham Lincoln elected to Congress	**1863**	Lincoln issues Emancipation Proclamation; delivers Gettysburg Address
1847-1849	Serves in Congress		

1850	Eddie Lincoln dies; William Wallace (Willie) Lincoln born		
1851	Thomas Lincoln dies	**1864**	Re-elected as president
1853	Thomas (Tad) Lincoln born	**1865**	Thirteenth Amendment passes Congress; Lincoln inaugurated for second term; Lee surrenders at Appomattox; Lincoln assassinated five days later, April 14, by John Wilkes Booth at Ford's Theater; April 15, dies; May 4, buried in Springfield
1854	Lincoln delivers first speech against the Kansas-Nebraska Act; re-elected to the legislature; resigns to run for U.S. Senate		

Part 3

Lincoln in Illinois

Almost Home

By Timothy P. Townsend, Historian,
Lincoln Home National Historic Site

By 1830, the Thomas Lincoln family was again on the move, this time to Illinois, where relatives had found rich farmlands. In March, they settled along the Sangamon River, eight miles west of Decatur. The following year, Lincoln hired himself out to take a flatboat loaded with produce to New Orleans. He successfully completed the trip in July 1831, but did not return to live with his family. Instead, twenty-two-year-old Abraham Lincoln set out on his own and settled in the Sangamon River village of New Salem, Illinois, about forty miles to the northwest of his parents' farm.

Within a year of Lincoln's arrival at New Salem, he began his political career by entering the race for the Illinois legislature. His campaign was interrupted, however, when he joined other volunteers in forming the 31st Regiment, Illinois Militia, at the beginning of the Black Hawk War, the war named for the leader of the Sac and Fox Indians, who fought against the United States Army and militia for possession of lands in northern Illinois and southern Wisconsin. The 31st Regiment elected Lincoln as their captain and he later recalled that he "has not since had any success in life which gave him so much satisfaction."

Lincoln, the public servant

Preceeding pages:
This engraving of the Lincoln home, titled "The Residence of Abraham Lincoln, President elect of the United States, at Springfield, Illinois" appeared in Frank Leslie's Illustrated Newspaper *on November 17, 1860.*

Some of the original furnishings, such as his desk, remain preserved in the Lincoln home.

Following an uneventful stint of military service, Lincoln returned to New Salem in July 1832. He made a last-minute attempt to win the legislative seat, but came in eighth out of thirteen candidates. The following year, he invested in a New Salem store, and was later appointed postmaster. In 1834, he took up land surveying and ran for the legislature again, this time winning. Lincoln took his seat in the state capitol at Vandalia. It was during this time that fellow legislator John Todd Stuart, also a native of Kentucky and a fellow Black Hawk war veteran, persuaded Lincoln to study law. Stuart also had a cousin in Lexington, Kentucky, named Mary Todd.

The Lincoln home, centerpiece of Lincoln Home National Historic Site, is being restored to its 1860s appearance. Rooms in the home, which contain some of their original furnishings, need only the visitor's imagination to evoke Lincoln as husband, father, politician, and president-elect. The Lincolns never sat together for a family portrait, but painter S. B. Waugh captured this domestic scene in 1866 *(lower left)* complete with a portrait of little Willie (who had died prior to its creation) hanging on the wall behind Robert Todd.

Lincoln wrote of his home in Illinois: "Here I have lived a quarter of a century, and have passed from a young to an old man."

One of Lincoln's earliest public opinions on slavery was recorded while he was serving in Vandalia. In 1837, a resolution came before the Illinois legislature in protest of abolitionism. Lincoln, with fellow legislator Dan Stone of Sangamon County, wrote a protest against the anti-abolitionist resolutions stating that they "believe that the institution of slavery is founded on both injustice and bad policy."

Lincoln was again elected to the Illinois legislature in 1836 and was elected three more times: 1838, 1840, and 1854, after his move to Springfield, although he would not serve the final term due to his subsequent bid for a seat in the U.S. Senate. Lincoln had moved to Springfield after playing a significant role in the move of the capital city from Vandalia. He and eight other Springfield area legislators—known collectively as the "Long Nine" because each was rather tall in height—won out over proponents for other cities for designation as the next capital. Lincoln concluded that his prospects were much brighter in the newly designated capital city and, in April 1837, he moved to Springfield to begin practicing law as a junior partner with John T. Stuart.

Lincoln arrived in town on horseback with everything he owned in two saddlebags. Springfield merchant Joshua Speed, also a Kentucky native born not far from Lincoln's birthplace, befriended him. Speed later recalled their first meeting when Lincoln came into Speed's store to inquire about the cost of a bed. When Lincoln admitted that he did not have enough money, Speed took pity on Lincoln and offered to share his own room above the store.

> "Where is your room?" asked he [Lincoln]. "Upstairs" said I, pointing to the stairs leading from the store to my room. Without saying a word, he took his saddle-bags on his arm, went upstairs, set them down on the floor, came down again, and with a face beaming with pleasure and smiles exclaimed "Well Speed I'm moved."

Lincoln lived with Speed until Speed moved back to Kentucky in 1841.

Springfield, Mary Todd, and home at last

The bustling town of Springfield was the largest that Lincoln had ever lived in, and he must have taken some satisfaction as he walked from Speed's store facing the public square at the southwest corner of Fifth and Washington streets, to the office of Stuart and

Lincoln in a newly constructed brick building one block north, knowing that he had a hand in bringing the capital and new found prosperity to Springfield. Raised as a frontier farm boy, Lincoln had the opportunity in Springfield to interact in a social circle of people with whom he had little prior experience, including one of Springfield's most prominent citizens, Ninian Wirt Edwards, the son of former Illinois governor Ninian Edwards. It was through Edwards and his wife, Elizabeth Edwards, that Lincoln would meet twenty-year-old Mary Todd, Elizabeth's sister visiting from Lexington, Kentucky.

From 1831 to the spring of 1837, Lincoln lived in New Salem, Illinois, in a cabin much like these re-created structures. In 1837, he left to practice law in Springfield.

Following an on-again, off-again courtship that nearly devastated the young suitor, Lincoln and Mary were married in the Edwards home on November 4, 1842. The newlyweds moved into the Globe Tavern, a two-story frame boarding house located on Adams Street, between Fourth and Third streets, in downtown Springfield. Within a week of the ceremony, Lincoln corresponded to a friend, "nothing new here, except my marrying, which to me, is matter of profound wonder." By May, Lincoln wrote to his friend Speed of "coming events": "I reckon it will scarcely be in our power to visit Kentucky this year. Besides poverty, and the necessity of attending to business, those 'coming events' I suspect would be some what in the way."

On July 26, Lincoln provided Speed with another short update, writing, "We are but two, as yet." That description would be inaccurate within days of its reporting, for Mary gave birth to Robert Todd Lincoln on August 1, 1843.

In late 1843, the Lincolns left the Globe Tavern and briefly rented a small house on south Fourth Street, between Monroe and Adams streets. But Lincoln's

Sites

1. Illinois State House
2. Site of Joshua Speed's Store
3. Site of William Butler House
4. Site of Simeon Francis House
5. Site of Ninian and Elizabeth Edwards Home
6. Site of Globe Tavern
7. Site of Lincoln's Rental Cottage
8. Lincoln Home, 1844–1861
9. Site of Sangamon County Courthouse
10. Site of Stuart and Lincoln Law Office, 1837–1841
11. Site of Logan and Lincoln Law Office, 1841–1843
12. Logan and Lincoln Law Office, 1843–1844
    Lincoln and Herndon Law Office 1844–ca 1852
    Tinsley Dry Goods Store
13. Site of Lincoln and Herndon Law Office, ca 1852–1865
14. The Marine Fire and Casualty Company
15. Governor's Mansion
16. Site of Corneau and Diller Drug Store
17. Site of Clark M. Smith Store
18. Clark M. and Ann Smith House
19. Site of Dr. William and Frances Wallace Hous
20. Site of First Presbyterian Church, 1843–1876
21. Site of Hutchinson Cemetery
22. Site of Illinois *Staats Anzeiger* newspaper of
23. Site of Illinois *State Journal* newspaper offic
24. Site of vacant lot that served as a "fives" co
25. Site of James C. Conkling Law Office
26. Site of Telegraph Office
27. Site of Chicago and Alton Railroad Depot
28. Site of John Williams and Company Store
29. Site of Illinois State Fairgrounds
30. Site of Springfield's Republican Wigwam
31. Site of Springfield's "Douglas Hall" or "The
32. Site of Watson's Saloon
33. Site of Chenery House Hotel
34. Site of Johnson Building
35. Great Western Railroad Depot

This map presents modern Springfield in relationship to places of note in historic Lincoln's Springfield. The numbered items represent the locations of places that Lincoln and his family knew, some of which still exist today. The inset map is a detail of Lincoln Home National Historic Site.

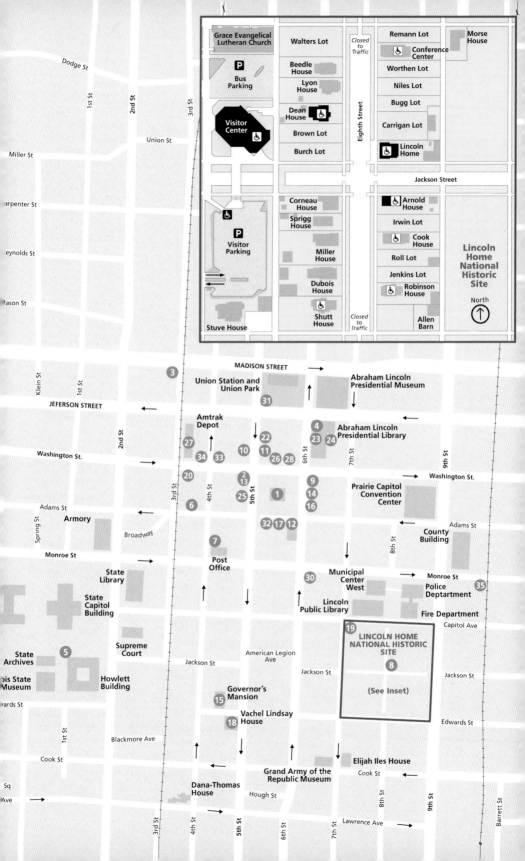

Mary Todd Lincoln was not the first "Mary" to whom Lincoln proposed. In the fall of 1836, the twenty-seven-year-old Illinois representative studying law agreed to marry one Mary S. Owens whom he had met three years earlier when she was visiting her sister in New Salem. Upon their second encounter some time later, though, she was not nearly as beautiful as he remembered. In fact, as he explained rather uncharacteristically unkindly to another friend, "I knew she was over-size, but she now appeared a fair match for Falstaff." In his letter to "Friend Mary" reproduced here, he seemingly assured her of his determination to marry but in reality gave her an opportunity to break their engagement. The poor first Mary detected his true feelings and rejected his proposal.

growing law practice soon provided the Lincoln family with the resources to purchase a home of their own. They found a small cottage at the northeast corner of Eighth and Jackson streets at the eastern edge of Springfield, and Lincoln began negotiations with the home's owner, Reverend Charles Dresser. Lincoln and Dresser agreed to a purchase price of $1,500 in cash and land transfer. In 1844, the Lincolns purchased the only home they would ever own. They moved in on May 1, 1844.

Lawyer, statesman, husband, father

His family settled in to their new home, Lincoln focused on his law business. John T. Stuart, Lincoln's first partner, was elected to the United States Congress in 1838 and won reelection in 1840. The demands of Stuart's office likely pulled him away from their law practice, often leaving Lincoln to run the firm alone. Their partnership ended in April 1841, and that same spring, Lincoln became a junior partner with Stephen T. Logan, another of Mary's cousins. Logan and Lincoln set up practice north of the square, across

Springfield in Lincoln's Time

Lincoln's Springfield in 1860 reflected a diverse mix of African Americans living in their own homes or with white employers, as well as immigrants from Germany, Ireland, and even a large contingent from Portugal. While no one knows exactly what Springfield was like in 1860, the illustration below suggests its appearance then. The Lincoln home was nestled in a heavily developed neighborhood. By the time the Lincolns left Springfield, there were houses all along Eighth Street, and the yards were filled with barns, sheds, privies, and gardens.

Metamora Courthouse, near Peoria, Illinois, was one of the Eighth Judicial Circuit courthouses in which Lincoln practiced law.

Fifth Street from where the Stuart and Lincoln offices were located. Two years later, they moved to the third floor of the Tinsley Building at the southwest corner of Sixth and Adams streets on the square. By 1844, Logan wished to set up practice with his son, so Lincoln invited one of their law clerks, William H. Herndon, to become Lincoln's junior partner, making Lincoln senior partner of his own firm for the first time. Lincoln and Herndon remained in the Tinsley Building until the 1850s, when they moved to the west side of the square. Lincoln became one of the most successful and sought-after attorneys in the state, and his client list included prominent individuals as well as corporations and powerful railroad companies. His cases ranged from property disputes and divorce to murder trials.

Lincoln had been practicing law for two years when Sangamon County became part of the Eighth Judicial Circuit. The state of Illinois was divided into judicial circuits so that rural communities had access to the legal system. The courts literally came to them, traveling to the various county seats in the spring and again in the fall. When the courts arrived, judges set up in a courtroom, which consisted of varying degrees of sophistication, and attorneys such as Lincoln would meet with their clients, sometimes just prior to their entrance into court. The communities took on a fes-

tive atmosphere when the courts came to town. The boarding houses filled up and, since many of the attorneys were also politicians, local citizens could count on speeches and lively political discussions. Lincoln took advantage of the circuit to enhance both his legal and political ambitions.

During the fall of 1844, Lincoln had the opportunity to campaign for Whig presidential candidate Henry Clay in the southern Indiana region where Lincoln spent his boyhood years. Lincoln's trip "home" must have stirred some feelings of his youth for, following his return, he wrote a series of poems inspired by his memories. The poems included imagery of his childhood home, the tale of a bear hunt, and the tragic story of a childhood acquaintance of Lincoln's named Matthew Gentry.

Lincoln's poetic expressions may have had other inspirations, for on March 10, 1846, Mary gave birth to their second son, Edward Baker Lincoln. Eddie was named for one of Lincoln's friends and colleagues, Edward D. Baker. It took several months, but Lincoln reported the blessed event to his old friend Speed, adding an update on the mischievous young Robert.

The new father's delay in informing Speed of Eddie's birth may have been due to Lincoln's campaign for the U.S. House of Representatives. Up to this time, Lincoln had served four terms in the Illinois legislature and had aspired to the Seventh District U.S. Congressional seat for several years. Because Whig voters dominated the district, three local Whigs—Lincoln, Edward Baker, and Jacksonville resident John J. Hardin (another of Mary's cousins)—agreed to take turns running for the Congressional seat to avoid possibly splitting the Whig vote to the benefit of the Democratic candidate.

Springfield merchant Joshua Speed befriended Lincoln when he arrived in Springfield with few resources and no place to live. The two developed a lifelong friendship.

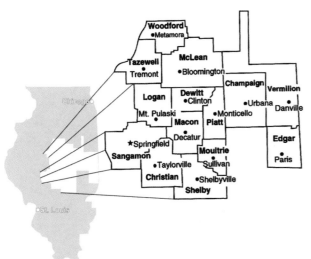

Lincoln was one of the few attorneys to regularly travel with the court as it went from county seat to county seat in central Illinois' Eighth Judicial Circuit, an area as large as the state of Maryland.

89

A. Lincoln: Attorney and Counselor at Law

John Todd Stuart *(right)* encouraged Lincoln to study law and was Lincoln's first law partner in Springfield. Lincoln's successful law practice grew to include large corporations, but he always maintained a broad client base that included more modest clients. This drawing *(below)* by an unknown artist depicts Lincoln's first law office, with Stuart, in 1837.

Lincoln's second law partner was Stephen T. Logan *(second from lower right)*. Lincoln was still a junior partner with this firm. The law firm of Logan and Lincoln moved into the Tinsley Building *(right)* at the southwest corner of Sixth and Adams streets in 1843. In 1844, Lincoln became a senior partner with William H. Herndon *(far right)*.

Lincoln's law practice even became the subject of campaign tactics, as illustrated by this mock business card most likely printed during his 1864 bid for re-election by his Democratic opponents announcing to his clients that he would "be back, on the same side from which I started, on or before the FOURTH OF MARCH NEXT, when I will be ready to swap horses, dispense law, make jokes, split rails, and perform other matters in a small way."

A. LINCOLN,

Attorney and Counselor at Law

SPRINGFIELD, - - ILLINOIS.

TO WHOM IT MAY CONCERN.

My old customers, and others, are no doubt aware of the terrible time I have had in CROSSING THE STREAM, and will be glad to know that I will be back, on the same side from which I started, on or before the FOURTH of MARCH NEXT, when I will be ready to SWAP HORSES, DISPENSE LAW, MAKE JOKES, SPLIT RAILS, and perform other matters in a small way.

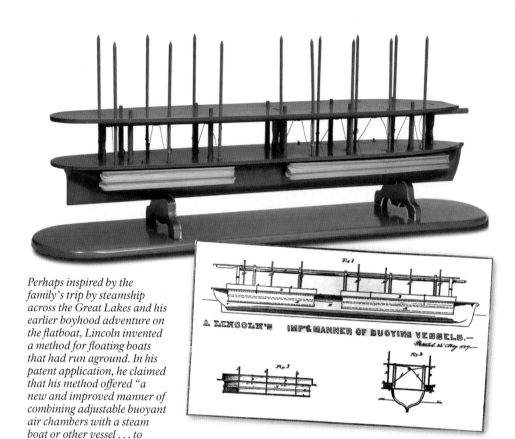

Perhaps inspired by the family's trip by steamship across the Great Lakes and his earlier boyhood adventure on the flatboat, Lincoln invented a method for floating boats that had run aground. In his patent application, he claimed that his method offered "a new and improved manner of combining adjustable buoyant air chambers with a steam boat or other vessel . . . to enable them to pass over bars, or through shallow water, without discharging their cargoes." Pictured here is a reproduction of the model and drawing required as part of the patent process. He was issued Patent 6469.

In 1846, it was Lincoln's turn to run. On election day, August 3, 1846, Lincoln won an overwhelming victory over his Democratic opponent.

The Lincolns in Washington

The Thirtieth Congress did not convene until December 1847. In the meantime, Lincoln continued his law practice and made plans for the trip to Washington. Lincoln and Mary decided that the entire family would live in Washington during the Congressional session and would travel to the capital city by way of Lexington, Kentucky, so that Mary could see her family. In October, Lincoln arranged to rent their home for one year to Cornelius Ludlum for $90 in a lease that stipulated that the Lincolns could store their furniture in the north upstairs room.

Once in Washington, Lincoln busied himself with affairs of Congress, while Mary, young Robert and Eddie were left to reside in Mrs. Sprigg's boarding house on the east side of the capitol building. Life in Washington must have proved disappointing for Mary. Largely confined to the boarding house looking after the boys, she had little female companionship since she was the only wife at the boarding house who accompanied her husband to Congress.

With the coming of spring, Mary likely had had her fill of life at Sprigg's and, perhaps at Lincoln's urging, returned to Lexington with the boys for the remainder of his first session. It didn't take long, however, for Lincoln to miss them. He wrote to Mary:

> In this troublesome world, we are never quite satisfied. When you were here, I thought you hindered me some in attending to business; but now, having nothing but business—no variety—it has grown exceedingly tasteless to me. I hate to sit down and direct documents, and I hate to stay in this old room by myself.

Mary, Robert, and Eddie had settled into her father's Lexington home, and she was again enjoying time with her family, receiving letters from Springfield, and traveling in and around the Lexington area. In May, she wrote to Lincoln about her activities, told him a story about the boys and a kitten, and expressed how much she missed him.

> Our little Eddy, has recovered from his little spell of sickness—Dear boy, I must tell you a story about him—Boby in his wanderings today, came across in a yard, a little kitten. [H]e brought it triumphantly to the house, so soon as Eddy, spied it . . . , he made them bring it water, fed it with bread himself, with his own dear hands . . . .
>
> How much, I wish instead of writing, we were together this evening, I feel vary [sic] sad away from you—
>
> I must bid you goodnight—Do not fear the children, have forgotten you—Even E eyes brighten at the mention of your name . . . .

Apparently the separation proved too much, for sometime during the summer of 1848, Mary and the boys returned to Washington and spent the rest of the summer there with Lincoln despite the city's oppressive heat. The House of Representatives adjourned on August 14, but Lincoln remained in Washington for several weeks working on behalf of Whig presidential candidate Zachary Taylor.

Hearth and home and heartache

In early September, Mary and the boys accompanied Lincoln on a speaking tour of New England on behalf

"In this sad world of ours, sorrow comes to all; and, to the young, it comes with the bitterest of agony, because it takes them unawares."

—A. Lincoln

"Love is eternal"

One of Springfield's most prominent citizens was Ninian Wirt Edwards *(upper right)*, the son of former Illinois governor Ninian Edwards. The Edwards home *(pictured below)*, prominently located at the western edge of Springfield on a small hill that overlooked the young town, was the site of many social functions attended by Lincoln. The junior Edwards' wife was Elizabeth Todd Edwards *(upper right)*. Her sister, twenty-year-old Mary Todd, visiting from Lexington, Kentucky, also enjoyed the grand affairs Elizabeth hosted in the Edwards home.

While it is not certain, Lincoln and Mary probably first met at one of the famous Edwards parties where many eligible bachelors visited and danced with young ladies. By 1840, Lincoln and Mary's relationship had advanced enough that they had apparently discussed marriage. How-ever, something happened to call off the engagement during the time Lincoln called "the fatal first of January," 1841. Lincoln was devastated with the breakup and fell into one of his bouts of depression that he referred to as "the hypo."

Fortunately, Abraham and Mary had supporters in Springfield who wished to see them reunited, and who worked on their behalf. Evidently they were successful, for in October 1842, Lincoln penned a poignantly personal letter to his friend Joshua Speed (who had since returned home to Kentucky), asking forgiveness for his impudence and inquiring of Speed's own recent decision to marry: "Are you now, in feeling as well as judgement, glad you are married as you are?"

Speed's reply must have encouraged Lincoln, for less than a month later,

Lincoln and Mary were again planning their wedding, which was to be in secret. Mary's niece, Katherine Helm, writing years later, perhaps provided one clue to the secrecy: "Mary wanted no advice, no more criticism of the man she loved."

The morning of the wedding, Lincoln visited the home of the Episcopal Reverend Charles Dresser and his wife Louisa *(lower right)*, at the corner of Eighth and Jackson streets (the same home that Lincoln would purchase in two years), to arrange for Dresser to officiate. Lincoln also ran into Mary's brother-in-law Ninian Edwards and told him of the couple's intentions. Edwards insisted that they be married in his home. Lincoln's other preparations that day included asking friend and fellow attorney James Matheny to be his best man. The groom also visited Chatterton's jewelry store on the west side of the public square to select a ring and have it engraved with the words, "Love is eternal."

Lincoln arrived at the Edwards home November 4, 1842, a bit before the ceremony that was to take place that evening. Lincoln and his best man, Matheny, stood in the Edwards parlor with Mary, who was dressed in white muslin and accompanied by her maid of honor, Julia M. Jayne. Reverend Dresser presided over the wedding witnessed by about thirty friends and family.

Lincoln sat for the photograph shown here *(at left)* in 1846 when he was congressman-elect. Mary also sat for her portrait *(second from left)* that same year. Robert Lincoln recalled years later that these companion portraits were "carefully preserved by my mother."

of Taylor. Toward the end of the month, on September 23, the family began a leisurely journey back to Springfield that included a sightseeing stop at Niagara Falls and travel aboard a steamship across Lakes Erie, Huron, and Michigan. They arrived in Springfield on October 10.

Their home was still occupied by their renter when the Lincolns returned home, so they stayed at the Globe Tavern. The overlap was likely intentional, for the first of several remodeling projects would soon make the home uninhabitable. Although it remained only a story-and-a-half tall, the home the Lincoln family returned to sometime during the spring or summer of 1849 had a new, spacious first-floor bedroom for Abraham and Mary.

Only months after settling back in, tragedy struck. First, word came to Mary that her father, Robert Todd, had died of cholera on July 16, 1849. Then her beloved maternal grandmother, Elizabeth Porter Parker, died six months later. Young Eddie Lincoln was also fighting for his life. Eddie had long been referred to as a "sickly" boy, but in December 1849, his illness was more serious. Mary cared for him as best she could as his fight against tuberculosis continued for 52 days. He finally succumbed at 6 a.m. on Friday, February 1, 1850.

The Lincolns' loss was tempered ten months later with the arrival of their third son, William Wallace, on December 21, 1850. Willie was named for Dr. William Wallace, who married Mary's sister Frances in 1839 and served as the family physician on occasion. The Wallaces lived at the corner of Seventh and Market streets, one block away from the Lincolns. The family greeted their fourth son, Thomas, or Tad as he was called, on April 4, 1853. Thomas was named for Lincoln's father who had died two years earlier on January 17, 1851, less then a month after Willie was born. Fido the dog completed the Lincoln family.

A need to serve

From 1849 to 1854, Lincoln did not hold an elective office, but instead gave speeches in support of other candidates and addressed issues of national importance such as slavery. Beginning with the Missouri Compromise of 1820, a series of laws maintained a tenuous balance of power between states that allowed slavery and those that prohibited it. However, the Kansas-Nebraska Act of 1854 superseded the Missouri Compromise by allowing the voters of the territories to decide if they would allow slavery into

Effects of the Fugitive-Slave-Law.

Holy Bible

Declaration of independence

their future state, infuriating many in the north who considered the compromise to be a long-standing, binding agreement. Lincoln stated that the repeal of the Missouri Compromise aroused him like never before, and he returned to political life with renewed vigor to fight a threatened expansion of slavery.

On November 7, 1854, voters elected Lincoln to the Illinois legislature. However, he resigned his seat when he learned that he could not hold that office and also run for U.S. Senate, his ultimate political goal. At this time, U.S. senators were selected from the state legislatures, rather than by direct vote of the people. By resigning, Lincoln could also more freely promote his candidacy, and he campaigned through the month of December in preparation for the convening of the legislative session that would elect the next senator.

Lincoln was in attendance at the state capitol for the legislative vote February 8, 1855, as was Mary, her sister Elizabeth, and half sister Emilie, who was visiting from Lexington. The ladies viewed the proceedings from the gallery of Representatives Hall. Lincoln had the highest number of votes on the first ballot, but not enough to win. Realizing as the subsequent balloting took place that he could not win, Lincoln threw his support to Lyman Trumbull, a Democrat

In September 1850, Congress passed a more restrictive Fugitive Slave Law that put greater requirements on authorities in the northern free states to assist with the return of escaped slaves and provided for the enlistment of civilians to aid in their capture. Free blacks were also at greater risk of being captured and sold into slavery. This print, published a month after the act's passage, depicts the ambush and shooting of four black men.

97

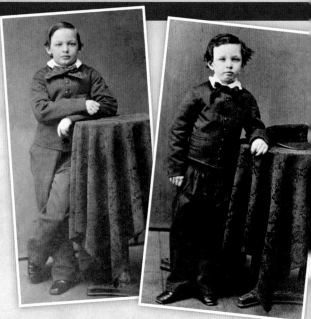

Family Life

Mr. and Mrs. Lincoln first set up household in a popular rooming house known as the Globe Tavern, where the Lincoln's first son, Robert Todd Lincoln *(pictured at far right)*, was born on August 1, 1843. This photo of the Globe Tavern *(below)* captured mourners gathered there at the time of Lincoln's funeral. The Lincolns welcomed their third son, William Wallace *(near left)*, on December 21, 1850. Their fourth son, Thomas, or "Tad" as he was nicknamed *(second from left)*, arrived on April 4, 1853. Both of the younger boys posed for their photographs in 1860.

The Lincolns indulged their children in a variety of ways. In late December 1859, Mary hosted a party to celebrate Willie's ninth birthday. She wrote out invitations stating that "Willie Lincoln will be pleased to see you, Wednesday afternoon at 3 o'clock." Pictured below is the invitation sent to young Isaac Diller, also shown.

Mary described Willie's party in a letter to Hannah Shearer: "Willie's birthday came off on the 21st of Dec. and as I had long promised him a celebration, it duly came off. Some 50 or 60 boys and girls attended the gala, you may believe I have come to the conclusion that they are nonsensical affairs. However, I wish your boys had been in their midst."

but someone who, like Lincoln, was opposed to the Kansas-Nebraska Act. Trumbull won, despite the fact that, on that first ballot, Lincoln had forty-four votes to Trumbull's five.

Lincoln continued his fight against the Kansas-Nebraska Act but, by 1856, he realized that he needed to abandon his beloved—but growingly ineffectual—Whig Party in favor of the rapidly expanding Republican Party that had become a force in Illinois. The national Republican convention took place in Philadelphia in mid-June 1856 and, in an early ballot, Lincoln received brief support as the vice presidential nominee. Ultimately, the new Republican Party selected famed western explorer John C. Frémont as its first candidate for president; William Lewis Dayton filled the ticket as the vice presidential candidate. Lincoln went to work campaigning for this first Republican presidential ticket with a series of speeches throughout Illinois. Despite the best efforts of Lincoln and the other Republican "Frémont Men," their candidate was defeated by James Buchanan.

Family time

With the Frémont campaign behind him, Lincoln spent more time at home. His opportunities to enjoy family and friends in Springfield had been rare since he maintained such an intense traveling schedule on the Eighth Judicial Circuit and the campaign trail, especially following passage of the 1854 Kansas-Nebraska Act. Later recollections by friends and family of Lincoln at home included scenes of him enjoying games such as chess and checkers.

Abraham and Mary were both avid readers as well, and Lincoln sometimes stretched out on the floor with an overturned chair as his back rest, reading aloud as Mary sewed. Mary's interest in literature was demonstrated in a reminiscence of her sister Emilie, who lived with the Lincolns for six months. Emilie recalled that Mary had read the novels of Sir Walter Scott to young Robert who reenacted one of the scenes in the yard.

> …one day hearing sounds of strife, we ran to the window. Bob and a playmate were having a royal battle. Bob with his sturdy little legs wide apart, was wielding a fence paling in lieu of a lance and proclaiming in a loud voice, 'this rock shall fly from its firm base as soon as I.' Mary, bubbling with laughter, called out 'Grammercy, brave Knights. Pray be more merciful than you are brawny.'

"Little Eddie"

The Lincolns welcomed their second son on March 10, 1846, and named him after Lincoln's friend Edward Baker. Although full of spirit, Edward Baker Lincoln, or "Eddie," was a sickly boy. He succumbed to tuberculosis on February 1, 1850, a month before reaching his fourth birthday.

Episcopalian Reverend Charles Dresser, the minister who had married Abraham and Mary, was not available, so Reverend James Smith, who had recently arrived at the First Presbyterian Church, came to console the Lincolns and officiated at Eddie's funeral at the Lincoln home at 11 a.m. on Saturday, February 2. Following the services, Eddie was buried in Hutchinson's Cemetery, eight blocks to the northwest of his home. The Lincolns notified the community of their loss in the small entry in the Illinois *Daily Journal (pictured at lower right)*. Several days later an anonymously submitted poetic tribute titled "Little Eddie" appeared in the same paper. Some scholars now attribute the poem to Lincoln.

After Eddie's death and the tender ministrations of Reverend James Smith, Mary Lincoln regularly attended the First Presbyterian Church *(pictured below)* at the southeast corner of Third and Washington streets where he was the pastor. Mary attended more regularly than Lincoln, who never officially joined but nevertheless rented a pew for the family. Many years later, Mary wrote to Reverend Smith that, "from the time of the death of our little Edward, I believe my husband's heart was directed towards religion."

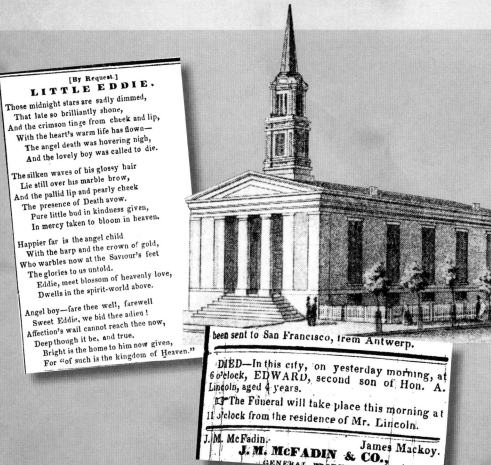

[By Request.]

LITTLE EDDIE.

Those midnight stars are sadly dimmed,
    That late so brilliantly shone,
And the crimson tinge from cheek and lip,
    With the heart's warm life has flown—
The angel death was hovering nigh,
    And the lovely boy was called to die.

The silken waves of his glossy hair
    Lie still over his marble brow,
And the pallid lip and pearly cheek
    The presence of Death avow.
Pure little bud in kindness given,
    In mercy taken to bloom in heaven.

Happier far is the angel child
    With the harp and the crown of gold,
Who warbles now at the Saviour's feet
    The glories to us untold.
Eddie, meet blossom of heavenly love,
    Dwells in the spirit-world above.

Angel boy—fare thee well, farewell
    Sweet Eddie, we bid thee adieu !
Affection's wail cannot reach thee now,
    Deep though it be, and true,
Bright is the home to him now given,
    For "of such is the kingdom of Heaven."

been sent to San Francisco, trem Antwerp.

DIED—In this city, on yesterday morning, at 6 o'clock, EDWARD, second son of Hon. A. Lincoln, aged 4 years.

☞The Funeral will take place this morning at 11 o'clock from the residence of Mr. Lincoln.

J. M. McFadin.

J. M. McFADIN & CO.,
GENERAL PRODUCE.

James Mackoy.

The Lincoln home was constructed in 1839, on a small knoll that rose slightly above the intersection of Eighth and Jackson streets, thus enhancing the appearance of the otherwise modest frame one-and-one-half-story cottage. It was constructed in a classic Greek Revival style with a front door centered between four windows. Entering the home, a visitor would stand in the center entry hall with the stairs to the small loft in front and slightly to the right. A room through the door on the left was probably a parlor, while a door to the right opened into what was likely a sitting room. The entry hall extended to the kitchen/dining room wing centered on the back of the house. The half-story loft included a center room at the top of the stairs with a small bedroom on either side. The peak of the ceiling was little more than six feet in height and quickly sloped down to each wall, leaving little room for someone of Lincoln's six-foot four-inch stature. The backyard contained outbuildings essential for a nineteenth century home, such as a summer kitchen/wash house, a barn for a horse and perhaps a cow and chickens, plus an outhouse.

The home would undergo several renovations as the Lincoln family grew and prospered. The first remodeling *(lower left)* in 1849 created another bedroom on the first floor, behind, or to the east of the front formal parlor. The upgrade also enclosed the open fireplace in the front formal parlor and replaced it with a heating stove. Although it remained only a story-and-a-half tall, the home now had a more spacious first-floor bedroom for Abraham and Mary. The Lincolns also changed the color from white to what was later referred to as "Quaker brown."

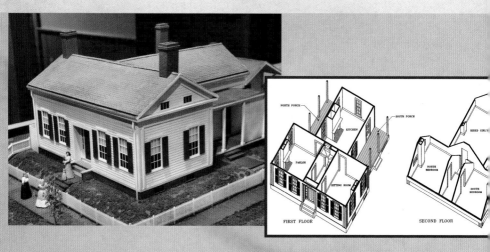

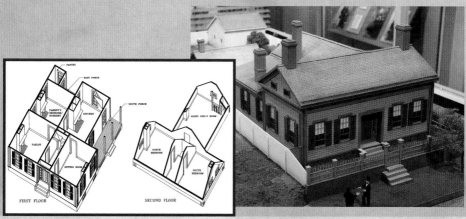

By 1855, with their family growing and with his legal career ever more successful, the Lincolns decided to enlarge their home again, this time adding a full second floor *(lower right)*. Mary may have provided the financial wherewithal to undertake such a large project, for she had received $1,200 for the sale of eighty acres of land her father had given her as well as approximately $1,000 from the settlement of her father's estate. The first phase of renovations added the second story above the front section of the house. The following year, the back of the house, or eastern wing, was enlarged. The work created enough space on the second floor so that all of the bedrooms could be moved there.

The small cottage that the Lincolns had lived in for twelve years had now almost doubled in size. It boasted a newly deco-rated and enlarged parlor that included the rear space that had been the first-floor master bedroom. The Lincolns now shared a bedroom suite on the second floor. The front upstairs space also included a spacious guest bedroom, and the rear wing included a bedroom for the boys as well as a room for domestic help. The kitchen wing was divided to create a separate dining room. Exterior work included extension of the brick retaining wall and construction of a high board fence along Jackson Street. With the home at last a more suitable size for the family and their finances, Mrs. Lincoln focused on the interior decor, creating a home that, while not the largest in Springfield, was certainly one of the most stylish.

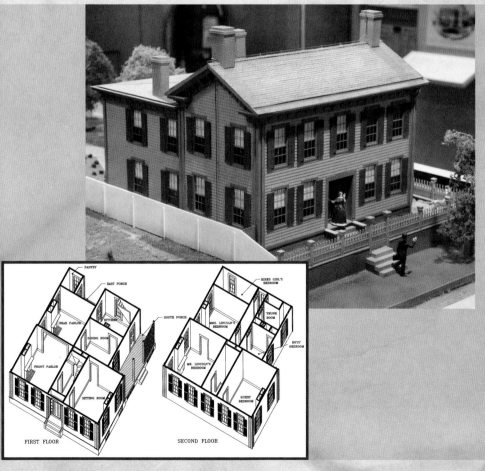

Friends and neighbors also recalled Lincoln's time with his children. A neighbor who lived to the east of the Lincolns commented that Lincoln would "take his children and would walk out on the rail way out in the country—would talk to them—Explain things Carefully—Particularly." He was often seen pulling young Willie and Tad in a wagon through the streets of Springfield and sometimes brought them with him to the law office on Sunday mornings when their mother was in church. Lincoln's law partner, Herndon, recalled his frustrations at his partner's indulgences with Willie and Tad: "His children did much as they pleased. Many of their antics he approved, and he restrained them in nothing . . .."

"In giving freedom to the slave, we assure freedom to the free. . . ."

—A. Lincoln

Slavery: "the great and durable question"

Lincoln and the Republicans barely had time to lick their wounds from their 1856 presidential defeat when they were hit with a turn of events that they saw as another step towards nationalism of slavery. On March 6, 1857, United States Supreme Court Chief Justice Roger Taney delivered the majority ruling in the case of Dred Scott v. Sanford, a decision that not only denied Dred Scott his freedom but also determined that African Americans were not citizens of the United States and therefore had no standing in the courts. The ruling further declared that, as property, slaves could be taken anywhere, ultimately concluding that the federal government did not have the right to prohibit slavery, a meaning that rendered the Missouri Compromise of 1820 unconstitutional.

The Dred Scott case put Lincoln in an awkward position. As an attorney, he spent his career supporting the judicial process and the rule of law. But Lincoln believed that Taney had gone too far when he said that the Declaration of Independence and the Constitution did not apply to African Americans.

Lincoln turned again to the U.S. Senate in 1858 to challenge Illinois Senator Stephen A. Douglas, who had championed the Kansas-Nebraska Act, for his Senate seat. In a show of unity, the Republican Party took the unusual step of nominating their candidate for Senate. On June 16, Lincoln accepted the Republican nomination and delivered what came to be known as his "House Divided" Speech in the Illinois Statehouse, warning, "A house divided against itself cannot stand. I believe this government cannot endure, permanently half slave and half free."

Opposite: *A set of dice, slates and carved animals are some of the toys exhibited in the boys' room*

Lincoln's absences from home while he was on the law circuit as well as campaigning proved to be a constant challenge for Mary. Having been raised in a wealthy Kentucky home, Mary was skilled in fine needlepoint and could speak French fluently, but she was less confident in the more mundane household chores. The Lincoln cottage, while a great leap forward for Lincoln, was something of a step back for Mary.

She took pride in her home and family, however, and worked hard to maintain the cottage, care for her children, and cook the family meals, which for several years was still done over an open cooking fireplace. One of Lincoln's remodeling efforts added the iron stove pictured below.

Like most middle class families of the day, Mary had a variety of domestic help to assist with the day-to-day care of the home. The daughters of local families worked for and lived with the Lincolns in the room pictured at lower left. They helped Mary run the household, while neighborhood boys helped with outdoor chores. Mariah Vance *(right)*, was employed by the Lincolns to help with the cooking and laundry but lived with her family not far away.

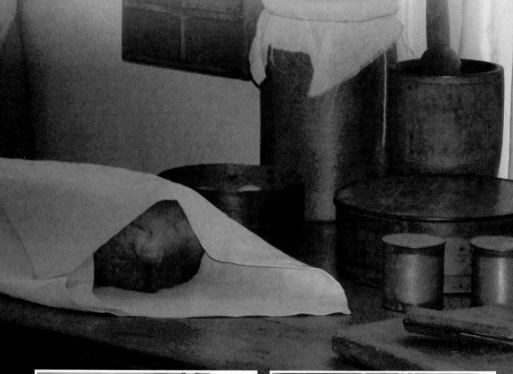

Lincoln wrote to Douglas with a proposal for joint meetings to discuss the issues publicly. They agreed to hold seven debates from one end of Illinois to the other, from August through October. This series of debates would capture the nation's attention throughout 1858 and have major implications two years later in the 1860 presidential campaign.

They met in towns in each of Illinois' congressional districts: Ottawa, Freeport, Jonesboro, Charleston, Galesburg, Quincy, and Alton, excluding Springfield and Chicago since they had already spoken there. Each debate was a major event. Thousands of people attended, listening to the two politicians debate for as much as three hours in whatever weather happened to occur, from the August heat to the chill of October. Douglas, the better known, better financed, and more influential of the two, often arrived with greater fanfare, but both were warmly received by their party faithful. The nation watched, and those who were unable to attend looked to their own party-affiliated paper for a "true" accounting of the proceedings. Reporters for the Democratic Chicago *Times* and the Republican Chicago *Press and Tribune* captured not only what was said by Lincoln and Douglas but also the spirit of the event.

Douglas maintained a consistent message throughout the debates, defending the Kansas-Nebraska Act and the notion of "popular sovereignty," or the right of citizens to decide the slave issue for themselves, and insisting that the nation's founders intended the Declaration of Independence and the Constitution for white people only. He appealed to the racism of the day when he associated Lincoln and the Republican Party with African American equality. Lincoln's consistent message throughout the debates was that the founding fathers intended that the Declaration of Independence and the Constitution applied to all.

At their final debate in Alton, Lincoln responded to Douglas' affirmation that the nation's founders did not intend to include African Americans in the Declaration of Independence. "I think the authors of that notable instrument intended to include *all* men, but they did not mean to declare all men equal *in all respects*. They did not mean to say all men were equal in color, size, intellect, moral development or social capacity. They defined with tolerable distinctness in what they did consider all men created equal—equal in certain inalienable rights, among which are life, liberty, and the pursuit of happiness."

Mary and Robert attended that final debate. They had taken a train from Springfield, with Robert traveling with a group of cadets who had formed during

"... there is no reason in the world why the negro is not entitled to all the natural rights enumerated in the Declaration of Independence, the right to life, liberty, and the pursuit of happiness."

—A. Lincoln in first debate with Stephen A. Douglas

Opposite: *Mr. and Mrs. Lincoln very much enjoyed each other's company and that of their boys in the sitting room pictured here.*

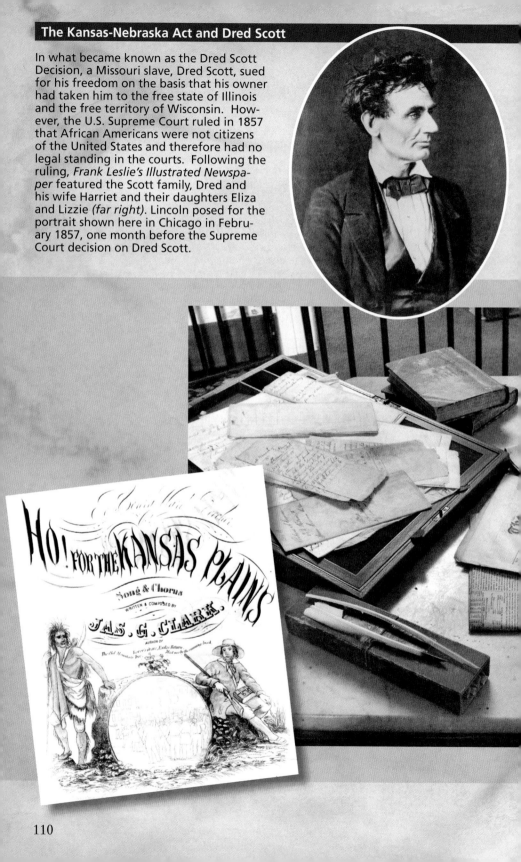

In what became known as the Dred Scott Decision, a Missouri slave, Dred Scott, sued for his freedom on the basis that his owner had taken him to the free state of Illinois and the free territory of Wisconsin. However, the U.S. Supreme Court ruled in 1857 that African Americans were not citizens of the United States and therefore had no legal standing in the courts. Following the ruling, *Frank Leslie's Illustrated Newspaper* featured the Scott family, Dred and his wife Harriet and their daughters Eliza and Lizzie *(far right)*. Lincoln posed for the portrait shown here in Chicago in February 1857, one month before the Supreme Court decision on Dred Scott.

In the meantime, the settlement of Kansas had been made more challenging and more violent with the passage of the Kansas-Nebraska Act of 1854. This act pitted pro- and anti-slavery settlers against each other in a sometimes bloody effort to control the ballot box. This song book cover (at left) shows a settler and American Indian and depicts a violent scene among settlers.

Lincoln considered the Kansas-Nebraska Act and the Dred Scott ruling as steps toward the nationalism of slavery. These issues spurred Lincoln to seek political office and to position himself to run against Stephen Douglas.

As his son Robert recalled, Lincoln was "a very deliberate writer, anything but rapid." He spent weeks working on various ideas, weaving in Shakespeare, mythology, and passages from the Bible as well as homespun humor to provoke the power of persuasion in his audiences. In the scene shown here re-created in the parlor of the Lincoln home, it appears as though the great orator has just stepped away from work on another speech.

In February 1855, the Illinois legislature met at the Illinois State House to select the person who would become the next U.S. senator from Illinois. Lincoln had worked hard to secure the Senate seat but withdrew his name from the race at the last minute and supported Democrat Lyman Trumbull, in a selfless move to prevent a supporter of the Kansas-Nebraska Act from winning.

the summer in Springfield. It is easy to imagine that fifteen-year-old Robert may have been distracted from the important discussions between his father and Senator Douglas with marching, drill and fun with his friends. His mother, however, with her deep interest in politics and pride in her husband, no doubt hung on every word of the three-hour debate, and she had every confidence in her husband even if he did not. Lincoln confided to a reporter about his fitness for the office, "I am convinced that I am good enough for it; but, in spite of it all I am saying to myself every day : 'it is too big a thing for you; you will never get it.' Mary insists however, that I am going to be Senator and President of the United States, too. Just think, of such a sucker as me as President!"

On election day, November 4, 1858, Illinoisans went to the poles to vote for the state legislators who would in turn elect the next United States senator when the new legislature convened in Springfield in January. Of necessity, Lincoln returned to his law practice following the campaign. As he wrote to Norman Judd in November, "I have been on expences [sic] so long without earning any thing that I am absolutely without money now for even household purposes."

Following the November election, but prior to the January legislative vote, Lincoln wrote his old friend and family physician Anson G. Henry, anticipating defeat: "I am glad I made the late race. It gave me a hearing on the great and durable question of the

age, . . . and though I now sink out of view, and shall be forgotten, I believe I have made some marks which will tell for the cause of civil liberty long after I am gone." The next day, despite Lincoln's comment to Henry that he would "sink out of view," he was looking to the future of the party, if not of himself. He maintained his fighting spirit and wrote a series of letters to colleagues and friends encouraging, "The fight must go on. We are right, and can not finally fail. There will be another blow-up in the so-called Democratic Party before long. In the mean time, let all Republicans stand fast by their guns."

On January 5, at 2 p.m., the Illinois legislature convened in a joint session in Representatives Hall for the election of the next U.S. senator. They selected Douglas over Lincoln by a narrow margin of 54 to 46.

In 1855, Lincoln wrote to his friend Joshua Speed, recalling an 1841 river trip they shared, and how the sight of slaves shackled together "was a continual torment to me." The photos here, taken during the Civil War, show a slave auction house in Virginia and five generations of a South Carolina slave family.

All for the party

Between law cases, Lincoln worked furiously to maintain party unity for the upcoming presidential contest. He wrote numerous letters and gave speeches whenever possible. He even bought a newspaper business to further the party voice. Understanding the importance to the Republicans of the immigrant vote in general and the German-Americans in particular, he purchased Springfield's German language newspaper, the Illinois *Staats Anzeiger*. In the contract, Lincoln retained the current editor to run the paper, but specified that it would be "a Republican newspaper, to be chiefly in the German language," and that it could not

The Great Debates

Lincoln delivered his "House Divided" Speech on June 16, 1858 in Representatives Hall of the statehouse, to kick off his race against Stephen Douglas for U.S. Senate. This image of the statehouse shows the west side. The Sangamon County Courthouse is in the far left.

Stephen Douglas *(near right)* maintained that settlement of the western states was the most important issue facing the nation, and that full equality for all was never the intent of the nation's founding fathers. Even though Lincoln lost the 1858 Senate race against Douglas, the debates brought him national notoriety. Lincoln sat for this portrait on October 1, 1858, having completed four of his seven debates with Douglas.

Following the debates, Lincoln arranged to have the transcripts published in book form *(right)*, which proved to be an asset to his 1860 presidential campaign.

print anything "opposed to, or designed to injure the Republican party."

During the summer of 1859, while her husband labored for the party, Mary kept busy entertaining. On June 26, she wrote to her friend Hannah Shearer about the events. "For the last two weeks, we have had a continual round of strawberry parties. This last week, we gave a strawberry company of about seventy. After raspberry time, we will resume, doubtless, our usual quiet."

The "usual quiet" became more pronounced, as Mary described in another letter to Hannah. "I am feeling quite lonely, as Bob, left for College in Boston, a few days since, and it almost appears, as if light & mirth, had departed with him." Robert left Springfield in August for Cambridge, Massachusetts, with his sights set on Harvard College. Unfortunately, Harvard's entrance exams proved too much for him. On September 15, 1859, he enrolled in Phillips Exeter Academy, a preparatory school. Robert received regular support from his father for tuition and expenses.

Lincoln was also gone a great deal during this time. He spent much of August through November 1859 on the road, traveling to Iowa, Ohio, Indiana, Wisconsin and Kansas, making speeches that continued his arguments against Douglas, popular sovereignty, and the expansion of slavery in an effort to bolster the Republican Party prior to upcoming state elections. He returned home long enough to celebrate Willie's ninth birthday that December but while Mary, Willie, Tad, and the rest of the children enjoyed the festivities, Lincoln was likely hard at work on yet another speech, one that would prove to be one of the most important of his career.

Lincoln's bookcase is still in the rear parlor of his Springfield home.

At Cooper Institute: A "passable" speech

Before he left for Kansas, Lincoln had received an invitation to speak at famed abolitionist Henry Ward Beecher's Plymouth Church in Brooklyn, New York. The recognition that Lincoln earned during his debates with Douglas and his recent speaking engagements prompted the invitation from the New York Republicans. They also had an interest in diluting the popularity of New Yorker William Seward, whom some had grown to dislike. By this time Lincoln had emerged as a contender for the 1860 Republican presidential nomination, and, while he was a long shot, he was beginning to think that he might just get it. Lincoln realized, however, that he was still not as well known

Opposite: *Lincoln's speech at New York's Cooper Institute on February 27, 1860, was pivotal in his bid for the presidency. Mathew Brady took this portrait of Lincoln while he was in New York to deliver the speech.*

Throughout the time they lived in Springfield, the Lincolns took their turns with other friends and neighbors at entertaining. Mary planned a large gathering for the evening of February 5, 1857, and with her husband's help, she wrote five hundred invitations. Mary reported on the affair to her sister, Emilie Helm, on February 16:

> Within the last 3 weeks, there has been a party, almost every night & some two or three grand fetes, are coming off this week . . . . I am recovering from the slight fatigue of a very large & I really believe a very handsome & agreable entertainment, at least our friends flatter us by saying so—About 500 were invited, yet owing to an unlucky rain, 300 only favored us by their presence, and the same evening in Jacksonville Col Warren, gave a bridal party to his son, which occasion, robbed us of some of our friends.

The Lincolns also took part, both as hosts and visitors, in the New Year's tradition when families would open their doors to visitors who would go from house to house throughout the day. In 1860, Mary wrote to her friend Hanna Shearer, "tomorrow I must rise early, as it is receiving day."

The Lincolns' restored formal parlor, shown here, looks much as it did when an artist for *Frank Leslie's Illustrated Newspaper* sketched the room in 1860 *(right)*.

as some Republican presidential hopefuls. His speech in New York would go a long way to getting him much needed exposure to the important eastern voters, and he spent hours researching and practicing.

Lincoln departed for New York on February 23, 1860, and arrived two days later. Upon his arrival, he learned that the event had been moved from Brooklyn's Plymouth Church to New York's Cooper Institute, so he made a few minor revisions to the text to reflect this altered venue from a church to an educational institution's lecture hall.

On the evening of February 27, frontier attorney Lincoln found himself standing before an audience of 1,500 skeptical New Yorkers. He rose slowly and began his remarks by making the case that the nation's founding fathers did not intend for the perpetuation of slavery. He then warned southern citizens that they were not justified in threatening to break up the Union over merely the election of a Republican president. Finally, Lincoln addressed the Republicans. "Wrong as we think slavery is, we can yet afford to let it alone where it is . . . ; can we, while our votes will prevent it, allow it to spread into the National Territories, and to overrun us here in these Free States? . . . Let us have faith that right makes might, and in that faith, let us, to the end, dare to do our duty as we understand it."

"No man ever before made such an impression on his first appeal to a New York audience," assessed a New York *Herald* reporter following Lincoln's speech. That same reporter also praised Lincoln's oration for its thoroughness in research and reasoning. Following

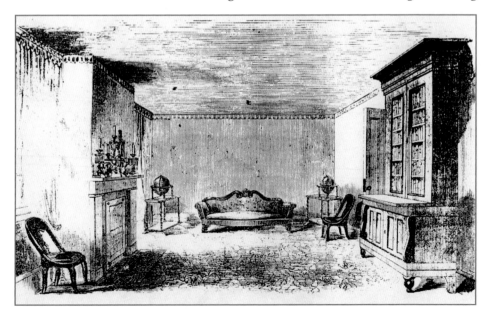

his speech, Lincoln went to the studio of famed photographer Mathew Brady and had a photograph taken that would prove to be a valuable campaign tool in the coming year.

Lincoln followed his Cooper Institute success with an intense speaking schedule, doing his best to accommodate as many requests as possible from Republican organizations throughout New England. On March 4, a weary Lincoln wrote Mary:

> I have been unable to escape this toil. If I had foreseen it, I think I would not have come east at all. The speech at New York, being within my calculation before I started, went off passably well and gave me no trouble whatever. The difficulty was to make nine others, before reading audiences who had already seen all my ideas in print.

Lincoln also took advantage of his time east for an extended visit with Robert at Phillips Exeter Academy in New Hampshire. At last, on March 12, Lincoln boarded a train in New York for his long awaited trip home and arrived in Springfield on the morning of March 14, at the Great Western Railroad depot at Tenth and Monroe streets. Springfield must have been a welcome sight, but Lincoln likely never

Above and opposite:
Lincoln received the official notification of his nomination for president in the rear parlor of his home, where the same sofa, chairs and many other furnishings remain preserved in the Lincoln home.

Lincoln became known as the rail splitter candidate. The slogan is attributed to Decatur politician Richard J. Oglesby, who located a fence in the Decatur area that Lincoln and his cousin John Hanks were said to have made in 1830. Hanks had roused enthusiasm for Lincoln when he had marched into the state convention in Decatur in early May 1860 with two split rails labeled:

ABRAHAM LINCOLN
The Rail Candidate
FOR PRESIDENT IN 1860
Two rails from a lot of 3,000 made in 1830 by Thos. Hanks and Abe Lincoln—whose father was the first pioneer of Macon County.

The cartoon pictured below (right) illustrates, through the use of the "Lincoln the rail splitter" imagery, that many in the south and some in the north associated Lincoln and the Republican Party with abolitionism or the immediate end of slavery.

The Republican National Convention opened in Chicago on May 16, 1860,

in a specially constructed building at Lake and Wacker streets that stood two stories tall and had a capacity of approximately ten thousand *(lower left)*. New Yorker William H. Seward was the front runner among the long list of hopefuls, but Ohioan Salmon P. Chase, Missourian Edward Bates, and Pennsylvanian Simon Cameron were also in contention. Lincoln was a minor candidate.

Lincoln did not attend the Chicago convention, but his advocates, including Jesse K. Dubois *(left)*, Jesse W. Fell, Ward Hill Lamon, Lyman Trumbull, Edward D. Baker, Norman B. Judd, and James C. Conkling *(right)*, all led by Lincoln's Eighth Judicial Circuit companion, Judge David Davis, went to Chicago to push his interests.

Conkling left the national convention early and returned to Springfield. As soon as Lincoln learned of Conkling's return, he went to Conkling's law office, located on the west side of Springfield's square *(as pictured below about 1859)* to learn of the events that transpired in Chicago.

Above and opposite:
Lincoln took advantage of the offer of use of the Governor's Reception Room at the statehouse to receive the many dignitaries and well wishers who wanted to see him. This room (opposite) *has been carefully restored at the Old State Capitol State Historic Site.*

imagined, as he stepped off the train, the coming year's events and the changes that would befall him, his family, and the prairie town that had been his home for twenty-three years.

The man who would be president

Once home, Lincoln again mixed law with politics, but this time he worked toward a presidential nomination. In April he wrote Lyman Trumbull about his feelings for the presidency, admitting, "The taste *is* in my mouth a little." The first step for the Lincoln campaign was the Illinois state convention, which opened in Decatur on May 9, 1860, in a specially constructed wood and canvas facility called the "Wigwam," a term popularly used for western Republican Party convention headquarters. Enthusiasm was very strong for Lincoln, although many of those attending the state convention felt that Lincoln would not win at the national convention. Nonetheless he received a unanimous endorsement.

While the Republicans worked to position themselves behind one candidate, the Democratic Party was splintering. The Democratic National Convention opened on April 23, 1860, in Charleston, South Carolina, but regional differences between northern and southern delegates resulted in adjournment without a candidate or a platform. To make matters worse, shortly after, on May 10, the newly formed National Union Party (from elements of the old Whig and American or "Know-Nothing" parties) nominated Tennessean John Bell. The Democrats tried again in June at Baltimore, but disagreement still raged and many of the southern delegates left in protest. The remaining delegates selected Stephen Douglas, while those delegates who boycotted the national convention met at another nearby venue and nominated John C. Breckinridge. The stage was set for a Republican victory.

The Republican National Convention opened in Chicago on May 16, 1860, at the national Wigwam. Lincoln did not attend, but instead remained in Springfield, anxiously awaiting the results. In an attempt to relieve some of his anticipation, Lincoln joined in a game of "fives," a variation on handball, in a vacant lot next to the Illinois *State Journal* office on the east side of Sixth Street, just north of the square. When Lincoln learned that James Conkling had returned from the convention early, he went to Conkling's law office, on the west side of the square, to learn what had transpired. Lincoln stretched out on a settee and carefully listened to Conkling's description of the convention, then stated "Well Conkling, I believe I will go back to my office and practice law."

"I hold that, in contemplation of universal law and of the Constitution, the Union of these states is perpetual."

—A. Lincoln

On August 8, 1860 a large Republican rally, complete with a parade and floats such as this re-creation *(below)* and artist's rendition *(left)*, wound through the streets of Springfield and stopped in front of the Lincoln home *(lower left)* on its way to the state fairgrounds. The rally included scores of "Wide-Awakes," a Republican marching club formed that same year to advocate "Free Speech – Free Soil – Free Men," preservation of the Union and the non-extension of slavery.

The Lincoln-Hamlin Ticket

The Republicans united behind the Abraham Lincoln and Hannibal Hamlin 1860 presidential ticket. Lincoln would not meet his vice president *(lower right)* until November 21, 1860, fifteen days after the election, when he and Mrs. Lincoln traveled to Chicago to meet the Vice President-elect and Mrs. Hamlin. The Lincolns and Hamlins held a public reception at the Tremont House hotel. Lincoln had also written to his old friend Joshua Speed asking if Speed and his wife would meet them in Chicago, so they enjoyed their company as well.

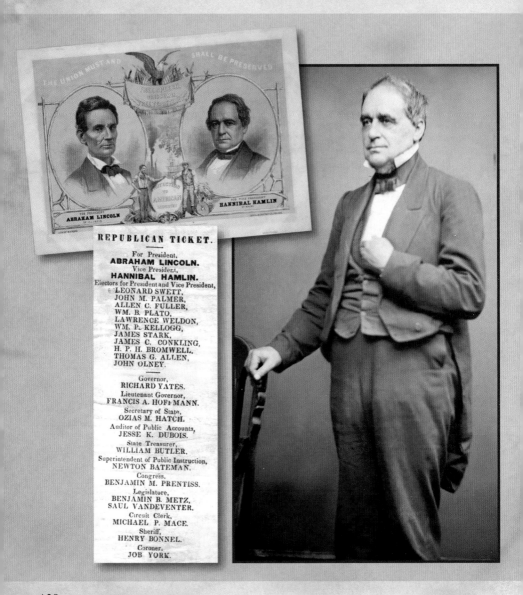

It would take three rounds of balloting on May 18, but, in the end, Lincoln received a unanimous nomination. The addition of vice presidential nominee Hannibal Hamlin, a former Democrat and eastern senator from Maine, balanced the Republican presidential ticket. After the first round, Lincoln had made his way to the telegraph office. As news came that he had won, he received the congratulations of all assembled there, then excused himself from the group, stating "Well, gentlemen, there is a little woman at our house who is probably more interested in this dispatch than I am."

Word of Lincoln's nomination spread quickly through Springfield. Guns were fired in celebration and friends called on the Lincolns at home all afternoon. A rally later that evening at the statehouse was followed by a marching band procession to the Lincoln home. The crowd called for Lincoln, who came to the doorway and credited this celebration as enthusiasm for the Republican Party rather than for himself. Lincoln then commented that he would invite the crowd into the house if it was large enough to hold them, but he welcomed as many as could find room. A member of the group anticipated the next presidential inauguration, shouting, "We will give you a larger house on the fourth of next March."

The following day, a large contingent from the Chicago Republican Convention traveled to Springfield by special train. An enthusiastic Springfield crowd greeted the train at the St. Louis, Chicago, and Alton station at Third Street between Jefferson and Washington streets, and formed a parade that included a Philadelphia band and two hundred of the conventioneers. The Springfield group, armed with split rails on their shoulders, escorted the new arrivals to the Chenery House hotel at the northeast corner of Fourth and Washington streets. The rest of the parade marched to the statehouse, one block east, for speeches.

A committee of ten from the convention, charged with officially notifying Lincoln of his nomination, proceeded to the Lincoln home where they were greeted by the Lincoln boys, Willie and Tad. When asked if he was Lincoln's son, Willie replied that he was, prompting Tad to speak up saying, "I'm a Lincoln too!" The delegation proceeded inside to the rear parlor where convention chairman George Ashmun read to Lincoln the formal notification of his nomination. Lincoln responded appreciatively and promised to provide a formal reply very soon. The delegation then adjourned to the sitting room where they visited with Mary and enjoyed ice water. Four days later, on May 23, Lincoln wrote Chairman Ashmun formally accepting the Republican nomination.

"Mr. Lincoln looked much moved, and rather sad, evidently feeling the heavy responsibility thrown upon him . . . . He replied briefly, but very pointedly. All appeared to have a foreboding of the eventfulness of the moment . . . ."

—Gustave Koerner in *Memoirs of Gustave Koerner* (recalling Lincoln as he received the Republican Party notification committee)

129

Lincoln realized the importance of making his image available for the presidential campaign and regularly indulged artists of various media. The Republican presidential nominee posed in front of his home for Boston photographer Adam Whipple. Whipple captured not only Lincoln *(in front of right window in photo of house below)* but also Willie and Tad and some of the neighbors in varying degrees of clarity. Tad is hiding behind the corner fence post, next to Lincoln.

In reply to an inquiry from New York for a photograph, Lincoln, referring to the Mathew Brady photo, suggested that the inquirer could "easily get one at New York. While I was there I was taken to one of the places where they get up such things."

Artists also painted, sketched, and sculpted Lincoln's likeness and captured images of the interior and exterior of his home. Leonard W. Volk, who had recently finished a sculpture of Stephen A. Douglas, had also created a life mask of Lincoln in his studio in Chicago in March of 1860. Volk visited the Lincolns at home just prior to the arrival of the nominating committee and presented Mrs. Lincoln with a cabinet-sized bust of her husband. Volk, pictured here with his bust of Lincoln *(top center)*, created castings of Lincoln's hands *(bottom center)* in the Lincoln dining room the day after Lincoln received the nominating committee. Volk recalled that May 18 visit and the castings that he did of Lincoln's hands the following day, on Sunday morning:

I found him ready, but he looked more grave and serious than he had appeared in previous days. I wished him to hold something in his right hand and . . . he went to the wood-shed . . ., and he soon returned . . . whittling off the end of a piece of broom-handle . . . . The right hand appeared swollen as compared with the left on account of excessive hand-shaking the evening before; this difference is distinctly shown in the cast.

Correspondence poured in after Lincoln's nomination, including the famed letter from New York schoolgirl Grace Bedell, who suggested Lincoln would get more votes "if you will let your whiskers grow."

Lincoln replied, "As to the whiskers, having never worn any, do you not think people would call it a piece of silly affection if I were to begin it now? Your very sincere well-wisher, A. Lincoln." A fully bearded Lincoln would be sworn in as president the following March. Before that time, attorney Lincoln was always clean shaven. This shaving mirror *(below)* is in Lincoln's bedroom and is thought to be the one he used there before he grew his famous beard.

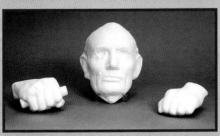

After his election, the Lincolns made arrangements with their neighbor, William Burch, to store some of their furniture in his home, which was directly across Eighth Street from the Lincolns. They also decided not to take their beloved dog Fido with them to Washington, leaving him instead with the Roll family who had children close to the ages of the Lincoln boys.

Life for the Lincolns and their Springfield neighbors would prove to be very exciting for the remainder of 1860. Political rallies by the Republican and Democratic clubs were held continually. By early summer, the Republicans were constructing a smaller version of the Chicago Wigwam on the southeast corner of Sixth and Monroe streets. Springfield's Wigwam was a circular frame building with a capacity of three thousand, and served as the venue for speeches by local Lincoln supporters and visiting dignitaries. The Democrats constructed their headquarters building at the northeast corner of Fifth and Jefferson streets. The new building was first known as Douglas Hall, after Democratic nominee Stephen Douglas, but was soon referred to as "The Barn." The name change was possibly due to the fact that Douglas was not the only Democrat running.

By June, Lincoln had taken advantage of Illinois Governor John Wood's offer of the use of the Governor's Reception Room in the statehouse, accommodations the New York *Herald* described as such that " . . . cannot be said to indicate the vast territorial extent of that commonwealth. It is altogether inadequate for the accommodation of Mr. Lincoln's visitors."

Life goes on

Despite the national spotlight, Lincoln did not excuse himself from family affairs. In late June, he bought a

pair of boots for his son Tad from John Williams & Company located on the north side of the square. The Williams' bookkeeper, anticipating a November victory, recorded the sale to "President Abraham Lincoln." Throughout July, the Republican nominee also took time to correspond with numerous friends, sharing simple news of his and the boys' health and Robert's impending entrance to Harvard. He even took time on July 22 to write a letter of encouragement to George Latham who, Lincoln learned in a letter from Robert, had failed the Harvard entrance exams.

Lincoln's routine never strayed far from the campaign, though, and in late July he met with German immigrant Carl Schurz, an outspoken opponent of slavery and chairman of the Wisconsin delegation at the Republican National Convention. Schurz busied himself campaigning for Lincoln and was in Springfield as the featured speaker at a July 24 statehouse rally. Schurz stayed at the Lincoln home and, after an evening visiting with the Lincolns, he and Lincoln were escorted to the statehouse by a torch parade featuring German and American "Wide-Awakes," young Republican club members who often marched in parades and attended rallies in military-style uniforms promoting Republican candidates.

The following month brought the highest level of excitement yet to the Lincoln home and neighborhood. Preparations had been ongoing for a large Republican rally that would take place August 8. The members of 21 Republican Wide-Awake clubs were on hand, and special trains brought 180 carloads of the Lincoln faithful to Springfield. The rally took place at the state fairgrounds, on the west side of the city, where speeches were given on five different platforms,

The day before leaving for Washington, Lincoln made one last visit to his law office, on the west side of the public square, to go over a few final details with his partner William Herndon.

"While it is true that the details of the private life of a public man have always a great interest in the minds of some—it is after all his works which make him live—& the rest is but secondary."

—Robert Todd Lincoln in *Herndon's Informants*

"Mary, Mary, we are elected!"

On election day, November 6, 1860, Lincoln left his statehouse office, crossed Sixth Street and entered Springfield's polling place in the Sangamon County Courthouse at the southeast corner of Sixth and Washington streets, where Lincoln had tried countless cases. The courthouse is shown in the engraving pictured below.

Lincoln cast his ballot for his preferred candidates in the day's other races, but removed his own name from the ballot. He then promptly returned to his office. Herndon, his law partner, recalled that initially Lincoln wasn't going to vote at all.

On the morning of election day I stepped in to see Mr. Lincoln, and was surprised to learn that he did not intend to cast his vote . . . but when I suggested the plan of cutting off the Presidential electors and voting for the State officers, he was struck with the idea, and at last consented. The crowd around the polls opened a gap as the distinguished voter approached, and some even removed their hats as he deposited his ticket and announced in a subdued voice his name, "Abraham Lincoln."

Lincoln then went home for dinner, and later that evening joined other

Republicans who filled Representatives Hall to await the election returns. Preliminary results began to arrive after seven o'clock but not quickly enough for Lincoln who, with Jesse K. Dubois and others, went to the telegraph office to get the results more quickly. The states of the Old Northwest reported first, in Lincoln's favor, but it was not until after eleven o'clock that all-important Pennsylvania went to Lincoln. The election seemed fairly secure, but Lincoln wanted to hear New York's vote. Time dragged and the group was invited to wait for the New York results at an establishment on the south side of the public square *(shown at center around 1859)* where the Republican ladies had supper waiting. It was there that Lincoln received the report that he had won New York, and it seemed that the whole town erupted in congratulations.

Mary had joined her husband at the statehouse to await the returns, and also attended the dinner, but had gone home prior to receiving the news from New York. At about 1:30 a.m. Lincoln proceeded home to announce, "Mary, Mary, we are elected!"

Mrs. Lincoln, Willie, and Tad posed for this photograph *(below)* in Springfield some time after the presidential election. *Frank Leslie's Illustrated Newspaper* published an engraving based upon the photograph to satisfy a public curious about President-elect Lincoln's family.

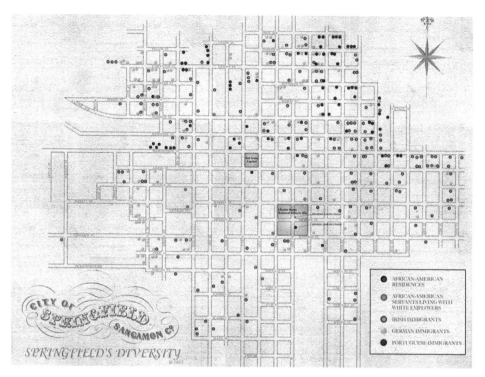

The various colored dots shown here reflect the diverse mix of residents in Lincoln's Springfield in 1860, including African Americans, as well as immigrants from Germany, Ireland, and even a large contingent from Portugal.

and lemonade and whole cooked steers were served. Upon his arrival, Lincoln's carriage was overrun with the throngs of supporters who carried him above the crowd to one of the platforms, where he made a few remarks. The rally also included a parade featuring a wide variety of floats that wound through the streets of Springfield and paused in front of the Lincoln home. Lincoln emerged dressed in a white suit and, while he declined to speak, he stood by the front door long enough for a photographer to capture the scene.

Election day

On election day, November 6, 1860, Lincoln felt confident of his chances to win, but would not know for sure until well after midnight when the results from New York finally came in. Despite his victory, a dark cloud hung over the election festivities, for Lincoln's name did not appear on most southern ballots. Not long after his election, Lincoln also learned that he was being hanged in effigy. Lincoln did not win a majority of the popular vote, and won his hometown by only sixty-nine votes. He actually lost Sangamon County (which includes Springfield) to Stephen Douglas.

Lincoln's activities as president-elect didn't change dramatically from his days as the Republican nominee, but his working hours did. The New York *Herald* reported on Lincoln's daily schedule: "Mr. Lincoln ... sometimes is even sooner ready for work than his private secretary, who sleeps in the building. . . . Light is seen in his room very late every evening, and he hardly ever allows anything to lay over unattended until the next day."

The increased workload proved too much for Bavarian-born John G. Nicolay, the twenty-eight-year-old secretary Lincoln had hired shortly after the nomination. Lincoln authorized the beleaguered Nicolay to hire additional help. Nicolay selected an old acquaintance, John Hay, who was in Springfield studying law under his uncle, Milton Hay.

"It will then have been proved that among free men there can be no successful appeal from the ballot to the bullet."

—A. Lincoln

Pressing appointments

Back in Springfield, Lincoln labored on cabinet appointments that had been committed in exchange for support, especially from important states such as Pennsylvania, Ohio, and New York. Lincoln's attentions were also diverted to the growing secession movement and talk of war, and while still in Springfield, he wrote numerous letters expressing his firm stance against the spread of slavery. Upon hearing that Congress was discussing compromise measures to alleviate the slavery crisis, Lincoln cautioned Illinois Senator Trumbull against allowing for the spread of slavery through Douglas' "popular sovereignty" as a solution:

> Let there be no compromise on the question of extending slavery. If there be, all our labor is lost, and, ere long, must be done again. The dangerous ground— that into which some of our friends have a hankering to run—is Pop. Sov. Have none of it. Stand firm. The tug has to come, & better now, than any time hereafter.

The tug came on December 20, 1860, when South Carolina adopted an ordinance of secession, breaking ties to the United States. The tension and uncertainty of the situation prompted Lieutenant General Winfield Scott, General-in-Chief of the United States Army, to bypass President James Buchanan and write directly to President-elect Lincoln in Springfield. The general's missive warned of the dangers of secession and predicted that the South would attempt to seize Southern forts prior to secession. One day after South Carolina's secession vote, Lincoln wrote from Springfield to Illinois Congressman Elihu Washburne with a message to pass along to General Scott that

Following Lincoln's election but even before leaving for Washington, he labored long on important correspondence and key cabinet positions that had been promised for support. New York Senator William Seward *(third from right)* was the favorite going into the Republican convention and visited Lincoln in Springfield in October 1860. In early December, Lincoln wrote to Seward asking him to accept the nomination for Secretary of State. He would also incorporate some of Seward's suggestions into his inaugural address.

Lincoln set aside most of December 15 for a meeting with Missourian Edward Bates *(second from right)*—another political leader who had supporters at the convention—who would ultimately serve as Lincoln's Attorney General. Other notables, such as New York political boss Thurlow Weed, met with Lincoln at his home in Springfield to discuss cabinet appointments. Lincoln also met with Pennsylvanian David Wilmot, the architect of the 1846 Wilmot Proviso (which aimed to ban slavery in land gained as a result of the war with Mexico) at Wilmot's hotel in Springfield on Christmas Eve. Wilmot was also offered a cabinet position but declined.

Edward D. Baker *(third from left)*, a former legal and political colleague of Lincoln and the namesake of Lincoln's second son, returned from Oregon where he had just won the election as U.S. senator to confer with Lincoln in Springfield. Baker would serve as one of two Senate escorts for the president-elect on the way to Lincoln's inauguration, and it was Baker who introduced "Abraham Lincoln, the President-elect of the United States" at the inauguration.

Simon Cameron

Edward D. Baker

Alexander Stephens

On December 30, Simon Cameron *(far left)*, another of the candidates for the 1860 nomination, arrived at the Lincoln home to discuss his cabinet potential. Lincoln had received numerous letters both in favor of and opposed to Cameron's appointment but needed to somehow appropriately recognize this powerful person from Pennsylvania. Cameron would fill the position of Secretary of War.

Ohio Governor and Senator-elect Salmon P. Chase *(fourth from right)* also had high hopes for his chances at the Republican convention. Chase arrived in Springfield in response to Lincoln's summons in January 1861, to talk about a cabinet position. Lincoln thanked Chase for his support during Lincoln's 1858 Senate race and offered

him the position of Secretary of the Treasury. Chase attended church with the Lincolns before returning home.

While still in Springfield, President-elect Lincoln responded to an urgent missive from Lieutenant General Winfield Scott *(far right)*, General-in-Chief of the United States Army, warning Lincoln that the South would try to seize southern forts prior to secession. Lincoln advised him to either hold or retake Federal forts that might come under Confederate attack.

Lincoln also corresponded with his old U.S. House of Representatives colleague, Alexander Stephens *(second from left)* of Georgia, about Southern secession and slavery. Stephens would soon become the Confederate vice president.

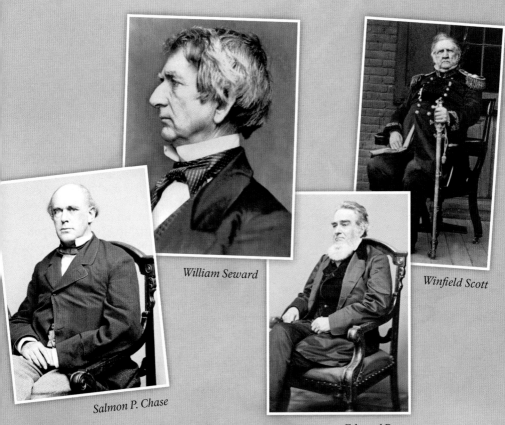

William Seward

Winfield Scott

Salmon P. Chase

Edward Bates

Lincoln would be "obliged to him to be as well prepared as he can to either hold, or retake the forts, as the case may require, at, and after the inauguration."

Even before being sworn in, the stress of these issues on Lincoln became apparent. The same day South Carolina adopted the secession ordinance, a New York *Herald* correspondent reported that "Lincoln's appearance has somewhat changed for the worse within the past week. He looks more pale and careworn," he added, "but, the vigor of his mind and the steadiness of his humorous disposition are obviously unimpaired."

In early February, Lincoln wrote a stern letter to William Seward, his newly chosen Secretary of State, that they should stay the course and not be tempted by compromise. Lincoln wrote, "I say now, however, as I have all the while said, that on the territorial question— that is, the question of extending slavery under the national auspices,—I am inflexible."

With his time in Springfield drawing short, Lincoln had vacated the Governor's Reception Room on December 28, 1860, with plans to spend most of his remaining time in Springfield at home. Lincoln also made arrangements for use of secluded space above his brother-in-law Clark M. Smith's store, on the south side of the statehouse square, to draft his inaugural address. Lincoln took his "First Draft" as he called it to the Illinois *State Journal* office to have it set in type. He then sent it to select colleagues for review. One of those reviewers was Seward, who suggested a slightly revised ending that Lincoln incorporated into what became his famous closing.

While Lincoln was working on his speech, Mrs. Lincoln, Clark M. Smith, and New Hampshire Congressman and Republican Party leader Amos Tuck embarked on a shopping trip to New York for supplies for the White House. Robert Lincoln joined the group in New York with plans to return to Springfield with his mother. Anxious for his wife's return, Lincoln went to the train station for three consecutive nights until Mary and Robert finally arrived on January 25. With his wife and son safely back, Lincoln made arrangements for a January 30 trip to see his aged stepmother and visit his father's grave in eastern Illinois.

Before he left for the visit to his stepmother, Lincoln placed an advertisement in the January 29, 1861, edition of the Illinois *State Journal* announcing the sale of some of the family furnishings. He also made arrangements to store some of the family's pieces at the home of William Burch, who lived across Eighth Street from the Lincolns. Lincoln announced that he would leave for Washington on February 11.

Two houses divided

In the midst of these last-minute details, word reached Springfield that seceded states had formed the Confederate States of America on February 4, 1861. Jefferson Davis was elected president and Lincoln's old congressional colleague, Alexander H. Stephens, was elected vice president.

Meanwhile, Mrs. Lincoln's efforts to provide a stylish and comfortable home for her family in Springfield had left an impression on visitors. The Republican National Convention's Chairman Ashmun reported, "I shall be proud, as an American citizen, when the day brings her to grace the White House." The Lincolns also endeared themselves to Springfield town folk and other honored guests by hosting one last reception on the evening of February 6, 1861, opening their door at 7 p.m. to over seven hundred visitors during a party that lasted well past midnight.

Two days after their farewell reception, the Lincoln family vacated their home of seventeen years and moved into the Chenery House for their last week in Springfield. They made arrangements to rent their home to Mr. and Mrs. Lucian Tilton for $350 per year. The Lincolns also left their beloved dog Fido in the hands of their friends, the Rolls, who lived at the southeast corner of Second and Cook streets.

One of the last details prior to his departure was setting his legal practice in order. Late in the afternoon of February 10, Lincoln returned, for a few moments, to his old law office. He and Herndon reviewed pending court cases and talked about old times. Herndon later recalled that last visit.

> He gathered a bundle of books and papers he wished to take with him and started to go; but before leaving he made a strange request that the sign-board which swung on its rusty hinges at the foot of the stairway should remain 'Let it hang there undisturbed,' he said, with a significant lowering of his voice. 'Give our clients to understand that the election of a President makes no change in the firm of Lincoln and Herndon. If I live I'm coming back some time and then we'll go right on practicing law as if nothing had ever happened.

On the morning of February 11, a carriage arrived at the Chenery House, driven by Lincoln's neighbor Jameson Jenkins, to take Lincoln to the train station. Lincoln, Robert, and the rest of the party left on the train ahead of Mary, Willie and Tad, who took another train and caught up to Lincoln later in the day.

African American drayman Jameson Jenkins drove Lincoln to the train station on the morning of Lincoln's departure for Washington. Jenkins, reportedly a conductor on the Underground Railroad, lived one block south of the Lincoln home. The house no longer stands, but is represented by an exhibit, disguised as a dray wagon, on the diversity of 1860 Springfield.

The Lincolns suffered in many ways during their years in Washington, but the hardest blow was the death of Willie (left) on February 20, 1862. This photo of Mary was taken one month prior to Willie's death, after which she went into deep mourning and only wore black for photographs during the remainder of the Lincoln presidency.

The first farewell

Despite the early hour, a crowd said to have numbered around one thousand gathered to see Lincoln off. He passed through the gathering of friends and neighbors, shaking hands with as many as he could, and then waited in the Great Western Railroad station for his departure. Just before 8 a.m., Lincoln climbed the train, turned and, addressing the gathering, reflected on his years in Springfield and the presidency awaiting him in Washington.

> My friends—No one, not in my situation, can appreciate my feeling of sadness at this parting. To this place, and the kindness of these people, I owe every thing. Here I have lived a quarter of a century, and have passed from a young to an old man. Here my children have been born, and one is buried. I now leave, not knowing when, or whether ever, I may return, with a task before me greater than that which rested upon Washington. Without the assistance of that Divine Being, who ever attended him, I cannot succeed. With that assistance I cannot fail. Trusting in Him, who can go with me, and remain with you and be every where for good, let us confidently hope that all will yet be well. To His care commending you, as I

hope in your prayers you will commend me, I bid you an affectionate farewell.

Lincoln's inaugural trip to Washington took twelve days, during which he made several stops and public appearances, including meeting in Westfield, New York, with young Grace Bedell who had written to Lincoln suggesting that he grow a beard. He arrived in Washington on February 23 and, on March 3, was inaugurated as the sixteenth president of the United States, thus beginning what would prove to be the most difficult presidency in history. Even during this time of crisis, with civil war on the horizon, Lincoln held out the hope for peace in his inaugural address: "...We must not be enemies. Though passion may have strained, it must not break our bonds of affection. The mystic chords of memory...will yet swell the chorus of the Union, when again touched, as surely they will be, by the better angels of our nature."

Lincoln sat for this photograph, the last known image of him, on February 5, 1865. He was assassinated by John Wilkes Booth while Lincoln and Mary were watching a play at Ford's Theatre on April 14, 1865.

His finest hours

This last-minute appeal failed to stop the approaching war, however, and on April 12, 1861, Fort Sumter in Charleston Harbor, South Carolina, was fired upon by the Confederacy. The fort surrendered two days later. The "house divided" crisis that Lincoln had predicted two years earlier had come to pass. In the ensuing years of his presidency, the terrible loss of life would bow him down, but none more than the death of young Willie, who died in the White House on February 20, 1862, probably of typhoid fever.

The remaining years would also prove his legacy, with the Emancipation Proclamation, the enduring Gettysburg Address, and the promise of reunification following the terrible Civil War. Following his re-election in 1864, Lincoln began to concentrate on reconstruction of the Union and life with his family following the presidency. On April 14, 1865, Good Friday, he and Mary took a carriage ride and remembered their son Willie who had died three years earlier. As Mary recalled, they also made plans for the future when they could perhaps travel and return to the quiet of their Springfield home. Lincoln seemed more cheerful than he had been in a long time. Later that evening, Lincoln and Mary attended a play at Ford's Theatre. At 10:30 p.m. Southern sympathizer John Wilkes Booth entered the presidential theater box, put a derringer pistol to the back of Lincoln's head and fired. Lincoln died at 7:22 a.m. the following day, just six days after Lee's surrender at Appomattox and a month after Lincoln's second inauguration.

"Frequent letters were received warning Mr. Lincoln of assassination, but he never gave a second thought to the mysterious warnings. The letters, however, sorely troubled his wife."

—Elizabeth Keckley in *Behind the Scenes*

In this pencil sketch by an unknown artist, Lincoln's body lies in state in the capitol in Springfield.

Opposite: *Lincoln's funeral train arrived in Springfield on May 3, 1865. Places associated with Lincoln's life were draped in mourning, including his home at Eighth and Jackson. Mourners also wore ribbons as a sign of their grief.*

One last journey, one final farewell

A shocked nation was thrown into mourning and, on April 21, 1865, after funeral services in Washington, the Lincoln funeral train, with Lincoln's remains and those of his son Willie, departed Washington and began a twelve-day trip back home to Springfield, largely reversing Lincoln's 1861 inaugural route.

The citizens of the United States responded with a variety of gestures, including eulogies, poems, songs and artwork, to express their feelings of grief. Cities located along the funeral route were draped in black. In Springfield, all of the major sites associated with Lincoln, including the statehouse, his law office, other downtown buildings, and especially the Lincoln home, stood shrouded in mourning.

The funeral train arrived in Springfield on May 3, and Lincoln's remains were placed in Representatives Hall, where he had given his "House Divided" Speech seven years earlier and where thousands of mourners now filed through. At 11:30 a.m. the following day, the Lincoln funeral procession, led by Lincoln's horse "Old Bob," left the statehouse and traveled south so that it passed the Lincoln home before turning north on its way to Oak Ridge Cemetery, where Lincoln and Willie were laid to rest, back home once again.

Lincoln home to be "forever free"

As part of the settlement of Lincoln's estate, Robert, his only surviving brother Tad, and their mother shared ownership of the Lincoln home. Upon Tad's death in 1871, his share of the home went to Mary. Robert eventually purchased his mother's share and continued to oversee and maintain the family home as rental property. Mary passed away in 1882, in the Springfield home of her sister Elizabeth Edwards, the same place where she and Lincoln courted and wed in 1842.

Robert eventually decided to donate his family's home to the state of Illinois as a memorial on the condition that it be well maintained and open free of charge to visitors. The Lincoln Homestead Board of Trustees was established in 1887 to "forever keep said Homestead in good repair and free of access to the public for the proper preservation of the property and relics and curiosities there collected."

By the 1940s, the impact of hundreds of thousands of visitors walking through the Lincoln home had taken its toll. The state planned a major restoration

Millions have made the pilgrimage to the Lincoln home since his funeral in 1865. An 1877 photo shows a group of visiting students *(right)*, while the 1950s image *(at left)* captures visitors traveling in open-air comfort. Although much of Springfield has changed, restoration work continues on the four-block National Historic Site, the centerpiece of which is the Lincoln family home of seventeen years. A walk through the neighborhood offers a glimpse of what Lincoln's Springfield was like when the Lincoln family lived here and provides some insight into the world that influenced our sixteenth president.

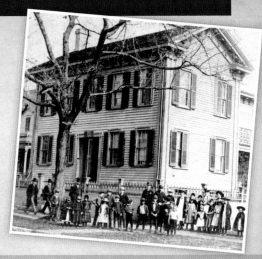

President Richard Nixon signed the legislation authorizing the establishment of Lincoln Home National Historic Site in the newly restored Old State Capitol State Historic Site on August 18, 1971. He used the desk that Abraham Lincoln sat at when working on his first inaugural address before leaving for Washington. Illinois Governor Richard J. Ogilvie (left) and Congressman Paul Findley (right) look on as President Nixon authorizes the creation of Illinois' only National Park.

of the home and, by 1951, archeologists were excavating the back yard to ascertain the locations of historic outhouses, barns, and other outbuildings. Restoration on the home itself began in 1952 and was completed by 1955.

National Park Service oversees major restoration

In the 1960s, new plans for the Lincoln home area were being developed that reflected a growing interest in historic preservation. It was decided that a residential neighborhood context was important when telling the Lincoln story, so plans incorporated a residential neighborhood feel immediately around the Lincoln home. The city of Springfield led an effort to close a portion of Eighth and Jackson streets to vehicular traffic, which was accomplished in 1964. But the overall task of restoring the Lincoln neighborhood and controlling commercialism proved too daunting without additional help. The National Park Service was approached in the late 1960s to study the possibility of acquisition of the Lincoln home and

the surrounding neighborhood. Legislation to create Lincoln Home National Historic Site was introduced into Congress in 1969, and President Richard Nixon signed the legislation in Springfield's recently restored Old State Capitol in 1971. One year later, the national historic site was officially established with the transfer of the Lincoln home from the state of Illinois to the federal government.

The National Park Service undertook a major restoration of the Lincoln home in 1988, creating a stronger, more stable, and more historically accurate Lincoln home reflecting its 1860 appearance. Today the Lincoln home is the centerpiece of Lincoln Home National Historic Site, revealing Lincoln as husband, father, neighbor, politician, and president-elect. It stands in the midst of a four-block historic neighborhood, which the National Park Service is restoring so that the neighborhood, like the house, will appear much as Lincoln would have remembered it.

This restoration, along with the humble beginnings preserved and reflected at the Lincoln Birthplace and Boyhood Home memorials, will help visitors better connect to the triumphs and tragedies of Abraham Lincoln and his family.

President Gerald Ford visited the Lincoln home on March 5, 1976, to dedicate the cornerstone for a new visitor center under construction. During his remarks, given from a podium in front of the Lincoln home, President Ford remarked that "It is to Abraham Lincoln that we owe the opportunity to observe our national bicentennial at peace among ourselves and with all nations."

Epilogue—"Part of Something Bigger"

"Knob Creek farm, the Rock [Sinking] Spring farm, Hodgenville, Elizabethtown, Muldraugh's Hill, these places he knew, the land he walked on, was all part of Kentucky. Yet it was also part of something bigger."

—Carl Sandburg

We often long to return to places of our past that were important to us. Lincoln was no different. While in Springfield, he wrote of his time in Kentucky and Indiana, and an especially emotional return to his boyhood home in Indiana inspired him to write poetry.

It is hard to imagine, though, that Lincoln could have predicted the amount of interest shown in the places where he lived. He might have gotten a hint of it on Sunday, April 9, 1865, while returning to Washington via the Potomac River aboard the *River Queen*. When the boat passed George Washington's Mt. Vernon home, a French diplomat who was with the president at the time remarked "Mount Vernon, with its memories of Washington, and Springfield, with those of your own home—Revolutionary and Civil War—will be equally honored in America." The comment prompted Lincoln to reply "Springfield, how happy I shall be four years hence to return there in peace and tranquility!" Unfortunately, Lincoln never returned to Springfield, but the Frenchman's comment proved very prophetic, for interest in Lincoln places matches or perhaps exceeds the interest shown in those associated with George Washington.

This interest is demonstrated through the desire by so many who want to "meet" Lincoln. Unfortunately, Lincoln admirers can no longer shake his hand, but they can put their hand on the stair rail that he used in his Springfield home; they can stand near the same Knob Creek that he played in as a young boy in Kentucky; and, they can visit the grave of his mother in southern Indiana. At these historic sites lives a sense of Lincoln glimpsed in the places where he grew, laughed, loved, and grieved. That is the power that these places have: the ability to take an icon like Lincoln and give him back to the people. Today's visitors come to the Lincoln sites from throughout the world, joining generations of people who have made similar visits, all becoming part of the history of those places and, hopefully, "meeting" Lincoln along the way.

Since his death at the hands of an assassin in 1865, the last casualty of the "terrible conflict," Abraham Lincoln has become an almost mythological figure

Abraham Lincoln

This portrait drawn by artist Joseph E. Baker around 1865 captures the immortal image of Abraham Lincoln.

in American history. Countless volumes have told and retold the story of his life and accomplishments, and numerous places are preserved because of their ties with his life. The National Park Service is proud to serve as the caretaker of several of these tangible connections with the boy, the man, the president, and the symbol of liberty and triumph over adversity that Abraham Lincoln has become.

In addition to the various archives of the three Lincoln sites featured in this guidebook, the following resources were consulted:

Books, pamphlets, journals:

Angle, Paul M. *Here I Have Lived: A History of Lincoln's Springfield, 1821–1865*. Chicago and New Salem: Abraham Lincoln Bookshop, 1971.

Baker, Jean H. *Mary Todd Lincoln: A Biography*. New York: Norton, 1989.

Barton, William E. *The Paternity of Abraham Lincoln: Was He the Son of Thomas Lincoln?: An Essay on the Chastity of Nancy Hanks*. New York: George H. Doran Co., 1920.

Basler, Roy B., ed. *The Collected Works of Abraham Lincoln*, 9 vols. New Brunswick, N.J.: Rutgers University Press, 1953–55. http://abrahamlincolnassociation.org (March 2007).

Bishop, Richard E. *The Nancy Hanks Lincoln Memorial*. Indiana Lincoln Union, 1944.

Dew, Charles B. *Apostles of Disunion: Southern Secession Commissioners and the Causes of the Civil War*. Charlottesville and London: University of Virginia Press, 2001.

Donald, David Herbert. *Lincoln*. New York: Simon & Schuster, 1995.

Fehrenbacher, Don E., ed. *Abraham Lincoln: A Documentary Portrait through His Speeches and Writings*. Stanford: Stanford University Press, 1964.

Gary, Ralph. *Following in Lincoln's Footsteps: A Complete Annotated Reference to Hundreds of Historical Sites Visited by Abraham Lincoln*. New York: Carol and Graff, 2001.

Helm, Katherine. *Mary, Wife of Lincoln*. New York and London: Harper & Brothers, 1928.

Herndon, William H., and Jesse W. Weik. *Herndon's Life of Lincoln*. New York and Cleveland: The World Publishing Company, 1942.

———. *Herndon's Lincoln*, 2 vols. Springfield: 1921.

Holzer, Harold, ed. *Lincoln As I Knew Him: Gossip, Tributes and Revelations from His Best Friends and Worst Enemies*. Chapel Hill: Algonquin Books, 1999.

Indiana Lincoln Union. *The Indiana Lincoln Memorial; Commemorating Lincoln's Mother and His Fourteen Years in Indiana*, 1938.

Johannsen, Robert W. *Stephen A. Douglas*. Urbana: University of Illinois Press, 1997.

King, Willard L. *Lincoln's Manager: David Davis*. Cambridge, MA: Harvard University Press, 1960.

Lupton, John A. "The Law Practice of Abraham Lincoln: A Narrative Overview. http://www.papersofabrahamlincoln.org/narrative_overview.htm (March 2007).

Miers, Earl S., ed. *Lincoln Day by Day: A Chronology, 1809–1865*. Washington, D.C.: Lincoln Sesquicentennial Commission, 1960. http://abrahamlincolnassociation.org (February 2007).

Neely, Mark E., Jr. *The Abraham Lincoln Encyclopedia*. New York: McGraw-Hill, 1982.

Pitcaithley, Dwight P. "Abraham Lincoln's Birthplace Cabin: The Making of an American Icon." *Myth, Memory, and the Making of the American Landscape*. Gainesville: University Press of Florida, 2001.

Pratt, Harry E. *Personal Finances of Abraham Lincoln*. Springfield, Illinois: Abraham Lincoln Association, 1943. http://abraham-lincolnassociation.org (February 2007).

Rankin, Henry B. *The Lincoln Life-Mask with some Comments and Corrections on Leonard W. Volk's Century Magazine Article.* Springfield, Illinois: Illinois State Historical Society, 1915.

Sculle, Keith A. "The Howard Family Legacy at the Knob Creek Farm." *Journal of the Abraham Lincoln Association* (Summer 2005). http://www.historycooperative.org/journals/jala/26.2/sculle.html (11 July 2006).

Tarbell, Ida M. *Abraham Lincoln and His Ancestors.* New York: Harper & Brothers, 1924.

———. *In the Footsteps of the Lincolns.* New York: Harper & Brothers, 1924.

Temple, Wayne C. *Abraham Lincoln from Skeptic to Prophet.* Mahomet, Illinois: Mayhaven Publishing, 1995.

———. *By Square and Compass: Saga of the Lincoln Home.* Mahomet, Illinois: Mayhaven Publishing, 2002.

Thomas, Benjamin P. *Abraham Lincoln: A Biography.* New York: Barnes & Noble, 1993.

Turner, Justin G. and Linda Levitt, eds. *Mary Todd Lincoln: Her Life and Letters.* New York: Alfred A. Knopf, 1972.

Villard, Harold G. and Oswald Garrison, eds. *Lincoln on the Eve of '61: A Journalist's Story by Henry Villard.* Westport, Connecticut: Greenwood Press Publishers, 1974.

Warren, Louis A. *Lincoln's Parentage and Childhood.* New York: The Century Company, 1926.

———. *Lincoln's Youth: Indiana Years, 1816–1830.* Indianapolis: Indiana Historical Society, 1991.

Wead, Doug. *The Raising of a President: The Mothers and Fathers of Our Nation's Leaders.* New York: Atria Books, 2005.

———. "The Shipley Ancestry of Lincoln's Mother." *Indiana Magazine of History* (1984). (Copy found in the Filson Club of Louisville, KY).

Wilson, Douglas L. *Lincoln's Sword: The Presidency and the Power of Words.* New York: Alfred A. Knopf, 2006.

Wilson, Douglas L., Rodney O. Davis, and Terry Wilson, eds. *Herndon's Informants: Letters, Interviews, and Statements About Abraham Lincoln.* Urbana: University of Illinois Press, 1998.

Unpublished works:

Blythe, Robert W. "Abraham Lincoln Birthplace National Historic Site: Historic Resource Study." National Park Service, Cultural Resources Stewardship, 2001.

Cultural Resource Division, SERO. "Abraham Lincoln Birthplace Memorial Building: Historical Structure Report." National Park Service, 2001.

Masterson-Brown, Kent. "Report on the Title of Thomas Lincoln to, and the History of, The Lincoln Boyhood Home Along Knob Creek in LaRue County, Kentucky." National Park Service, 2003.

Peterson, Gloria. "An Administrative History of Abraham Lincoln Birthplace National Historic Site: Hodgenville, Kentucky." National Park Service, Division of History, Office of Archeology and Historic Preservation, 1968.

Santosuosso, John E. "A Survey of Lincoln Boyhood National Memorial and Lincoln City." National Park Service, Lincoln Boyhood National Memorial, 1970.

Acknowledgments

The National Park Service expresses its appreciation to all the persons who made the preparation and production of this handbook possible. All photos and artwork not credited below come from the files of the National Park Service. Some materials from park files are restricted against commercial reproduction.

The authors are grateful for and would like to acknowledge the talent and extra effort put forth on this book by Editor Diana L. Bailey and Graphic Designer Amy Thomann with the Donning Company Publishers. Thanks also go to Eastern National for sponsoring the project.

Cover and p. 48: Young Lincoln courtesy Library of Congress

p. 6: Lincoln portrait courtesy Library of Congress

pp. 8–9: Bernard Wall subscription serial drawing reprinted by permission of the Abraham Lincoln Library and Museum at Lincoln Memorial University, Harrogate, TN

pp. 14, 43, 82: Lincoln Trail Map reprinted by permission of Lincoln Financial Group

pp. 16–17: Copy of marriage certificate reprinted by permission of Old Fort Harrod State Park and Kentucky Department of Parks; Ostendorf artwork reprinted by permission of Carl Howell

p. 19: Children at well reprinted by permission of Cecilia Broderick

pp 20–21: Logs on wagon courtesy Library of Congress

pp. 24–25: Historic Lincoln Tavern reprinted by permission of Mary Brooks Howard

p. 28: James Howell photo, post card reprinted by permission of Carl Howell

p. 31: Theodore Roosevelt and inkwell photos reprinted by permission of Sagamore Hill National Historic Site

pp. 32–33: Centennial coin and ribbon reprinted by permission of Lincoln Library and Museum at Lincoln Memorial University, Harrogate, TN

pp. 44–45: Tools, cabinet courtesy University of Chicago Library, Lincoln Collection, Library of Congress; Nancy Hanks Lincoln painting reprinted by permission of Lloyd Ostendorf family; Thomas Lincoln photo courtesy Library of Congress

p. 48: J. L. G. Ferris painting courtesy Library of Congress

p. 51: White snakeroot photo by G. A. Cooper reprinted by permission of Smithsonian Institution

p. 53: Copybook page, firelight painting courtesy Library of Congress

p. 61: Young Lincoln illustration reprinted by permission of Lloyd Ostendorf family

pp. 74–75: Centennial poster reprinted by permission of Lincoln Library and Museum at Lincoln Memorial University, Harrogate, TN; Lincoln family, David Gilmour Blythe painting of Lincoln courtesy Library of Congress

p. 78: Desk photo by Donna Lounsberry

pp. 80–81: Lincoln home, neighborhood, rocking chair, Mary Lincoln bedroom, and fireplace photos by Donna Lounsberry; family portrait courtesy Library of Congress

p. 83: Cabins at New Salem photo by Donna Lounsberry reprinted by permission of Looking for Lincoln Heritage Coalition

p. 86: Letter courtesy Library of Congress

p. 87: Lincoln home, barn photos by Donna Lounsberry

p. 88: Metamora Courthouse reprinted by permission of Abraham Lincoln Presidential Library

p. 89: Joshua Speed photo reprinted by permission of Abraham Lincoln Presidential Library

pp. 90–91: Law office engraving reprinted by permission of The Lincoln Museum, Fort Wayne, IN; Tinsley Building engraving, John Todd Stuart, William H. Herndon and Stephen T. Logan photos reprinted by permission of Abraham Lincoln Presidential Library; business card courtesy Library of Congress

p. 92: Patent drawing reprinted by permission of The Lincoln Museum, Fort Wayne, IN

pp. 94–95: Lincoln and Mary photos courtesy Library of Congress; Elizabeth and Ninian Edwards photos reprinted by permission of Abraham Lincoln Presidential Library

p. 97: Fugitive slave print courtesy Library of Congress

pp. 98–99: Willie, Tad and Robert Lincoln photos reprinted by permission of The Lincoln Museum, Fort Wayne, IN; birthday invitation and Globe Tavern photo reprinted by permission of Abraham Lincoln Presidential Library

p. 101: First Presbyterian Church engraving reprinted by permission of Abraham Lincoln Presidential Library

pp. 102–103: Home model photos by Donna Lounsberry

p. 104: Boys' room photo by Donna Lounsberry

pp. 106–107: Kitchen and hired girl's room photos by Donna Lounsberry, Mariah Vance photo reprinted by permission of Abraham Lincoln Presidential Library

p. 108: Sitting room photo by Donna Lounsberry

pp. 110–111: Lincoln photo, song book cover, and Frank Leslie's newspaper courtesy Library of Congress; Lincoln's papers photo by Donna Lounsberry

p. 112: Old State Capitol photo reprinted by permission of Old State Capitol State Historic Site

p. 113: Slave family and slave auction house photos courtesy Library of Congress

pp. 114–115: Old State Capitol, Stephen A. Douglas and Lincoln photos reprinted by permission of Abraham Lincoln Presidential Library

p. 116: Lincoln photo courtesy Library of Congress

pp. 118–119: Parlor photo by Donna Lounsberry

p. 121: Rear parlor photo by Donna Lounsberry

pp. 122–123: James C. Conkling photo reprinted by permission of Abraham Lincoln Presidential Library; Chicago Wigwam photo reprinted by permission of The Lincoln Museum, Fort Wayne, Indiana; Springfield square photo reprinted by permission of Sangamon Valley Collection, Lincoln Library, Public Library of Springfield, IL; political cartoon courtesy Library of Congress

p. 124: Engraving reprinted by permission of Abraham Lincoln Presidential Library

p. 125: Reception room photo reprinted by permission of Old State Capitol State Historic Site

pp. 126–127: Rally photo reprinted by permission of Abraham Lincoln Presidential Library, parade float photo by Donna Lounsberry, certificate courtesy Library of Congress

p. 128: Campaign banner, poster, and Hannibal Hamlin photo courtesy Library of Congress

pp. 130–131: Lincoln home and Leonard Volk photos reprinted by permission of Abraham Lincoln Presidential Library

p. 133: Law office engraving reprinted by permission of The Lincoln Museum, Fort Wayne, IN

pp. 134–135: Mary, Willie, and Tad photo and courthouse engraving reprinted by permission of Abraham Lincoln Presidential Library; Springfield square photo reprinted by permission of Sangamon Valley Collection, Lincoln Library, Public Library of Springfield, IL

pp. 138–139: All portraits courtesy Library of Congress

p. 141: Jenkins wagon photo by Donna Lounsberry